Vietnam: The Endless War

VIETNAM:
The Endless War

From *Monthly Review*, 1954-1970

by Paul M. Sweezy, Leo Huberman, and Harry Magdoff

New York and London

Contents

Preface

Nearly everyone would probably agree that nothing in the last quarter century has had a more traumatic or decisive effect on the United States, as a nation and as a society, than the war in Vietnam. All the more remarkable, therefore, is the almost total failure of the recognized social sciences in the United States, or for that matter in any part of the Western world, to come up with a coherent explanation of the origins of the war, the issues over which it is being fought, and its probable future course.

It is not the purpose of this small volume to probe the roots of this failure, which lie deeply imbedded in the social and intellectual history of the last two centuries or more. We want rather to demonstrate in as concrete a way as possible that failure to understand what the war in Vietnam is all about is not in the least inevitable, that from a Marxist perspective there is not now, and never has been, any mystery about the origins of the war, its steady escalation over the years, and its persistence in the face of official America's repeated avowal of a will to bring it to an end.

In order to make this demonstration as convincing as possible, we eschew reliance on hindsight. The book consists solely of editorial statements which appeared in MONTHLY REVIEW beginning in 1954 and ending in 1970. No changes of substance—i.e., beyond technical editing—have been introduced. The editorials are reproduced just as they were written, usually timed as commentary on the war's many turning points, and the date of publication, indicated on the first page of each, should be noted by the reader. Individually and collectively these pieces carry their own story and require no clarification or elaboration here.

Since these are editorial rather than individual statements, it is relevant to note that the first eight were written when Leo Huberman and I were co-editors of MONTHLY REVIEW, the ninth when I alone was editor, and the last two since Harry Magdoff has joined me as co-editor. This explains why all three of our names appear on the title page.

—Paul M. Sweezy

New York City
August 1970

What Every American Should Know About Indo-China

The war in Indo-China really began nearly a hundred years ago. It was in 1858, according to the standard sources, that France began the long process of imposing colonial rule on the country, and colonial rule has always implied more or less continuous warfare between rulers and subjects.

Sometimes the struggle is little noticed in the outside world, but it is rarely absent. Take, for example, Laos, which is now part of Indo-China and over which the French established a "protectorate" toward the end of the nineteenth century. In French textbooks, the Laotians are described as the very model of a lazy and contented native people who are supposed to need and appreciate the benevolent rule of civilized nations. And yet, according to a recent study, "the history of these fifty years [of French rule] shows a long series of popular uprisings, tirelessly conducted by this 'amiably indolent' people who are 'satisfied with their lot.' "*

Sometimes, on the other hand, the struggle reaches the level of full-scale warfare, as it has during the last eight years in Indo-China—though not for the first time. The following description of warfare in Tonkin (northern Vietnam) might almost be from yesterday's paper. Actually, it is from the *Encyclopedia Britannica's* accounts of events which transpired in the years 1884-1891:

The people of Tongking began to rise. The occupation of Tongking became a prolonged warfare, in which 25,000 French, compelled to guard innumerable posts, had to oppose an intangible enemy, appearing by night, vanishing by day, and practising brigandage rather than war. The military expenditure, met neither by commerce, which had become impossible, nor taxation, which the

---

* Jean Chesneaux, "Le Laos sort de l'ombre," *Cahiers Internationaux,* May 1953, p. 84.

Annamese could not pay nor the French receive, resulted in heavy deficits. Than-quan, Hon-Koi, Lao-Kay, Pak-Lun and Kao-Bang were occupied, but the troops were driven back to the Delta and almost invested in the towns. [Successive Residents General] were all powerless to deal with the uninterrupted "bush-fighting" and the augmentation of the deficit for no sooner was the latter covered by grants from the mother country than it began to grow again. The rebels held almost all the delta provinces, their capitals excepted, and from Hanoi itself the governor general could see the smoke of burning villages at the very gates of his capital. (Omissions are not indicated.)*

That time the fighting lasted some six years; this time it is already in its eighth year. It has been going on so long, in fact, that there is a danger we shall forget how it started and perhaps even fall for Mr. Dulles' fairy stories about the gallant French and their allies, the Associated States of Indo-China, fighting an uphill battle against the wicked aggression of "Communist imperialism." If you live among madmen you may sooner or later begin to accept their delusions as real. The only way to save yourself is to stop every so often and have a look at the sober facts of the real world.

Indo-China in World War II

When France fell in 1940, the colonial regime in Indo-China decided to collaborate with Japan just as the Vichy government decided to collaborate with Hitler. In both countries a patriotic resistance movement grew up which assisted the allied cause and in turn received material and military aid, particularly from the American Office of Strategic Services. In Indo-China, the resistance was called the Vietminh, which is an abbreviation of the Vietnamese for "League for the Independence of Vietnam." It was led from the beginning by Ho Chi Minh, a veteran revolutionary who had been in the thick of the fight for Vietnamese independence before and during World War I and who had subsequently founded the Vietnamese Communist Party. By the end of World War II, the Vietminh had gained complete mastery over a number of provinces in north-

---

* *Encyclopedia Britannica*, 13th ed., Art. "Indo-China, French," Vol. 14, pp. 493-494.

east Indo-China and thus had established a solid territorial base, much as the Chinese Communists had in China.

As the war approached an end in Europe, the French in Indo-China, seeing the handwriting on the wall, began to plan to throw out the Japanese and change sides again. But the Japanese beat them to the draw and in March 1945, locked up all French military and civilian personnel, proclaiming Vietnam to be an "independent" state under the Annamite Emperor Bao Dai.

When the Japanese surrendered in August, the French were in jail and the resistance movement, amid great popular enthusiasm, assumed power without even a struggle. Bao Dai, far from putting up a fight, quietly abdicated his throne and (under his civilian name of Vinh Tuy) accepted a position as "Supreme Councillor" to the Ho Chi Minh government. Early in September, a new state, the Democratic Republic of Vietnam, declared its independence. Four months later, the first and only free general elections in Vietnamese history gave a crushing majority to Ho Chi Minh and his colleagues: in Hanoi their slate won 98.4 percent of the votes.*

The end of World War II, so it seemed, marked the end of French rule in Indo-China and the birth of a new Vietnamese state.

The Trouble Begins

But things were not so simple as they first appeared to be: they rarely are. The French had no intention of staying out of Indo-China, and it soon turned out that they had powerful friends to help them return.

At the Potsdam Conference in July 1945, it had been decided (on whose motion?) that the responsibility for disarming the Japanese in Indo-China should rest with the Chinese in the region above the 16th parallel and with the British in the south. The Chinese army that came down from the north was

---

* By this time, the French had seized control in the south so that the voting in that region had to be secret. So far as we know, however, no one disputes the fact that the result of the election as a whole was an overwhelming victory for the Vietminh regime.

actually not a Kuomintang army; it was a regional Yunnanese army which Chiang Kai-shek was anxious to get out of the way in order to facilitate the consolidation of his own control over Yunnan, a province that up to then had remained relatively autonomous. The Yunnanese showed no particular interest in the internal affairs of Vietnam and on the whole helped to consolidate the power of the Ho Chi Minh government.

It was very different in the south. There, the British General Gracey was in charge, and it was his policy to restore imperialist rule and no nonsense. To quote the *New Statesman & Nation* (April 17, 1954): "General Gracey not only refused to deal with Ho Chi Minh's government, claiming—absurdly—that it was a Japanese puppet; but he armed French troops, freed from Japanese internment, disarmed the Vietminh, declared martial law, and made use of Japanese troops to maintain law and order." The newly elected Labour government in London, to its everlasting shame let it be said, promptly put the stamp of approval on this policy by signing an agreement with France turning the area over to French control. General Leclerc, named commander of an expeditionary force by de Gaulle, brought in fresh troops and proceeded to "pacify" the area.

Vietnam was now effectively split into two parts. The seeds of the future war had been sown—not, it should be emphasized, by the Russians (who were nowhere near Indo-China) nor by the Chinese (who respected the right of the Vietnamese to manage their own affairs) nor by the Americans (whose policy in Asia still reflected Roosevelt's strong distaste for colonialism of the kind practiced by the French) but by the British. It is one of those ironies of which history seems to be so fond that the British, who subsequently were to have the good sense to withdraw from India and Burma, were responsible for shoehorning the unregenerate Dutch and French back into Indonesia and Indo-China.

Dirty Work

While restoring their hold on the South, the French began to maneuver to get back into the North as well. The methods they used were guile, deceit, and ultimately brute force.

The immediate French problem was twofold, to get the Chinese to agree to evacuate the country and to get the Democratic Republic of Vietnam to permit French forces to enter the North (particularly the Red River Delta with its capital city of Hanoi and its seaport of Haiphong). This problem was solved by simultaneous negotiations in Chungking and Hanoi. The French High Commissioner, Admiral Thierry d'Argenlieu, went to Chungking, while his deputy M. Sainteny went to Hanoi. The key to the success of both negotiations was what seemed at the time to be an enormous concession by the French to the Vietnamese: they recognized the new Republic. Here is the agreement, signed by Sainteny and Ho Chi Minh on March 6, 1946:

1. The government of France recognizes the Republic of Vietnam as a free state *having its government and its parliament, its army and its finances,* forming part of the Indo-Chinese federation and of the French Union. Regarding the reunion of the three "Ky" [that is Cochin China in the south, Annam in the center, and Tonkin in the north], the French government agrees to be bound by the decisions of the peoples consulted by referendum. [Emphasis added.]

2. The government of Vietnam agrees to receive in a friendly fashion the French army when, in accordance with international agreements, it comes to relieve the Chinese troops.

3. The foregoing stipulations will become effective immediately. Directly after the exchange of signatures, each of the high contracting parties will take all necessary measures to bring about a cease fire on the battlefields, to maintain their troops in their respective positions, and to create a climate favorable to the immediate opening of friendly and frank negotiations. These negotiations will be related particularly to:

    a) diplomatic relations of Vietnam with foreign states;
    b) the future status of Indo-China;
    c) French economic and cultural interests in Vietnam.*

It should be remembered that the "French Union" had not yet been defined at this time, but the italicized clause in the first paragraph—"having its government and its parliament, its army and its finances"—proves conclusively that Ho Chi Minh was promised a wide and genuine degree of independence, ap-

---

* The text of the agreement is taken from Paul Rivet, "Le Drame Franco-Vietnamien," *Cahiers Internationaux,* June 1949, p. 46.

proaching if not equalling that enjoyed by the British Dominions.

Having signed the accord, Ho embarked for France to negotiate the matters detailed in the third paragraph. On March 18, Leclerc's army entered Hanoi.

Immediately, the French regime in Indo-China, under the direction of Admiral d'Argenlieu, began to violate and undermine the agreement—deliberately and without the slightest doubt for the purpose of reducing all of Indo-China once again to the status of a colony. On June 1, 1946, a puppet regime was set up in Cochin China in evident violation of the promise to abide by the results of a popular referendum. French troops were sent into areas under Vietnamese control, despite the promise to maintain the military status quo. And during the summer, d'Argenlieu convoked a conference to which he invited representatives of Cochin China, Laos, and Cambodia but *not* representatives of the legally recognized Vietnamese government. Both the pattern and the purpose were obvious to everyone.

It has been said that these high-handed acts of the French colonial authorities were taken behind the back, and even in direct contravention to the orders, of the government in Paris (which at that time, it will be recalled, included both Communists and Socialists). No doubt they were taken behind the backs of some (perhaps most) of the members of the government, but it is certain that Paris must share the guilt of its emissaries in Indo-China. What happened prior to and at the Fontainebleau conference between Ho Chi Minh and the French government during the summer of 1946 proves that beyond any possibility of doubt. *The French deliberately planned to torpedo the conference with a view to undermining and ultimately overthrowing the Ho Chi Minh government.*

Here is the testimony of Professor Paul Rivet who was asked to serve as a member of the French delegation to the Fontainebleau conference:

The French delegation was presided over by M. Max André, who was my colleague on the General Council of the Seine and is now [1949] a Senator for the Seine. I have the greatest esteem for this affable and courteous colleague. . . . Nevertheless, it is certain that the choice of M. Max André could not please the Vietnamese who were not ignorant of his connections with the Banque franco-chinoise and hence with the Banque of l'Indochine.

. . . M. Max André invited all the French delegates to his house on July 5, 1946, for the purpose of getting together before the first official Franco-Vietnamese conference scheduled for the next day. I accepted this invitation. I was surprised not to find among the delegates anyone who I knew had a profound knowledge of Indo-China. . . . I asked at the opening of the meeting for the text of the accords of March 6th which should serve as a basis for the discussions and which I hoped to be able to study that evening. My question seemed to be inopportune, and I was informed that these texts would eventually be communicated to me. On the other hand, there was much insistence on the necessity for strict discipline in the delegation and for strict observance of decisions arrived at by the majority of its members. From this moment, I kept silent. I listened to the proposals exchanged among the delegates and, on taking leave of M. Max André, I announced that I was resigning.

That same evening, I communicated this decision to M. Marius Moutet [Minister for Overseas Territories] in a long letter in which I said that I did not intend to be a dupe nor an accomplice nor a hostage, and in which I denounced the grand-style maneuver which was to be pursued for many months with a rare tenacity: to lead the Fontainebleau conference into an impasse, to profit from the discredit which the failure of the negotiations was supposed to cast upon the negotiators, particularly on Ho Chi Minh, and to propose (and if need be impose) the Bao Dai solution while depriving Tonkin of rice from Cochin China and thus provoking a famine.

M. Marius Moutet certainly did not believe in this machiavellian plot. He did not acknowledge receipt of my letter. Desiring to publish it, I asked him for it. He states that he left it in the archives of the ministry, and a search made there has yielded no result. Mystery!*

Or rather, no mystery at all. M. Moutet may have been as stupid as Professor Rivet paints him. But *somebody* in Paris knew the score, and it was manifestly the same score known to Admiral d'Argenlieu in Saigon.

How the War Began

When Ho Chi Minh left France in September 1946 he signed a so-called modus vivendi with Moutet, but naturally

---

* *Ibid.,* p. 47.

enough it failed to settle any of the crucial issues and Ho must have known that the French were determined to destroy his regime. If he had any doubts on the subject, they were soon to be dispelled.

Even while the Fontainebleau conference was in session, the French in Indo-China had launched the operation which they counted upon to deliver the *coup de grâce* to the Republic. The year 1945 had been one of famine in Tonkin: at least a million persons, and possibly twice that number, died of starvation. Under the circumstances, Ho's government was forced to suspend collection of land taxes, and for the time being it was left with only one effective source of revenue, customs collected at the port of Haiphong. (An interesting sidelight on French policy: despite the enormous profits made by the Banque de l'Indochine and a handful of other French monopolies operating in Indo-China, absolutely no taxes were collected from these companies. The Republic, of course, was precluded from imposing such taxes until the appropriate agreements had been negotiated with France.) During the summer of 1946 the French set out to substitute French for Vietnamese control of the customs in Haiphong. Success, obviously, would enable them to suffocate the Republic financially and, if need be, literally to starve it to death. All this, of course, despite the March 6th agreement recognizing the Republic as a "free state . . . having . . . its finances."

Beginning July 26th, when "the French maritime authorities notified the Chinese authorities that henceforth Chinese ships touching Haiphong will be subject to French control,"* the French steadily extended their encroachments on the prerogatives and activities of the Vietnamese administration in Haiphong. The Vietnamese, for their part, resisted to the best of their ability while maintaining a conciliatory attitude and obviously hoping to be able to adjust matters peacefully. Nevertheless,

---

* Quoted from official documents by H. Lanoue, "Comment a debuté la guerre du Viet-Nam: le massacre de Haiphong (23 novembre 1946)," *Cahiers Internationaux,* November 1952, p. 73. This is a detailed and completely documented study of the beginning of the war by an engineer who was chief of personnel at the Saigon arsenal in the years 1946-1948.

incidents increased in number and seriousness, culminating in pitched battles in the streets of Haiphong on November 20th and 21st.

The fighting, which had been aggressively extended by the French commander in Haiphong, Colonel Debès, was brought to a halt by a cease fire arranged between the French authorities in Hanoi and the Vietnam government (which had its capital in Hanoi). Colonel Lami, who represented the French in the cease-fire negotiations, addressed a letter to Colonel Debès in which he stated:

Every effort must be made to avoid the outbreak of a conflict which would immediately become general and which would endanger not only the isolated French posts in Haiphong and Vinh but also the [French] civilians in Hanoi.*

This, however, was not the attitude of the French authorities in Saigon. On September 21st, while the cease-fire negotiations were in progress, General Valluy, commander of all French forces in Indo-China and acting High Commissioner (Admiral d'Argenlieu was then in Paris), sent the following telegram to Colonel Debès:

Following Haiphong events of the 20th deem indispensable to profit from incident to improve our position Haiphong. Have given following instructions to General Morlière [commander at Hanoi and Debès superior officer]: Guarantees to be obtained after quick inquiry are: Primo: Evacuation Haiphong by all regular and paramilitary Vietnamese armed forces. Secundo: Complete freedom for our troops to take up positions in the city.†

General Morlière, who received the same instructions, replied to General Valluy the same day as follows:

In receipt of your telegram at the same time that am informed Colonel Debès has heard directly from you through COMAR [Commandant de la Marine]. To demand complete evacuation of Haiphong by regular and paramilitary Vietnamese forces is to decide with all certainty, I repeat with all certainty, on the conquest of the city which should be preceded, if huge losses are to be avoided, by its partial destruction by artillery. It is tantamount to complete

---

* *Ibid.*, p. 77.
† *Ibid.*, pp. 77-78.

rupture of the accords of March 6 and of the *modus vivendi* [signed by Ho Chi Minh and French Overseas Minister Moutet] and to the almost certain extension of fighting to all our Tonkin garrisons. Deem it my duty to indicate these probable repercussions. . . .*

In the face of this warning, in direct contravention of the cease fire which had just been agreed upon, and in the absence of any new incidents, General Valluy telegraphed direct to Colonel Debès the message which was to touch off the war:

It appears clearly that we are facing premeditated aggressions carefully prepared by the Vietnamese army which seems no longer to obey its government. In these circumstances your honorable efforts at conciliation and division of cantonments are no longer admissible. The moment has come to give a rude lesson to those who have traitorously attacked us. By all the means at your disposal you should make yourself complete master of Haiphong and force the Vietnamese government and army to make amends. . . . You will confront President Ho Chi Minh with his overwhelming responsibilities and with the grievous consequences which can result from his attitude toward the French government.†

Was General Valluy acting on his own or was he following orders from Paris? On the basis of the evidence that has been published to date it is impossible to say. After a careful study of known facts, Henri Lanoue, from whose excellent article on the origins of the war we have been quoting, is forced to confess his inability to answer the question. His final word on the subject is perhaps worth quoting:

Some day it will be necessary for the responsible government leaders of that period to say whether orders to act were given by them, or whether they allowed their hands to be forced by the initiatives of Valluy-Debès and others. If this second explanation should be offered, it would be hard to understand why no inquiry was ever undertaken and why no punishment—quite the contrary—was ever meted out to originators of these initiatives.‡

However this question is finally decided, there is no possible room for doubt that responsibility for the opening of hostilities rests squarely on the French side and not on the Vietnamese.

---

* *Ibid.*, p. 78.
† *Ibid.*
‡ *Ibid.*, p. 84.

On the morning of November 23rd, Colonel Debès delivered two ultimatums to the Vietnamese authorities in Haiphong and, on being told that they were standing on the cease-fire agreement of the 21st, gave the order for operations to commence. Shells and bombs were poured into the defenseless city from land, sea, and air. The number of civilians killed that day was put at 20,000 by the Vietnamese; French authorities admit to 6,000.

After that, of course, it was war. Fighting broke out here and there immediately, and on December 19th the people of Hanoi rose against the French, killing forty-three in the course of the uprising. The French government and colonialists have always tried to fix responsibility for the war on this supposed "aggression" of the Vietnamese—with what justification we leave it to the reader to judge for himself. In any case, the state of war became general after December 19. The government of the Republic, knowing now what it was up against, retired once again to the hills and began to prepare for the long struggle ahead.

Efforts to End the War

This does not mean that Ho Chi Minh's government *wanted* to fight a war. The whole record from the very beginning shows that it wanted to negotiate a settlement with the French and that in order to do so it originally was quite prepared to concede France a special position—economically, culturally, and politically. It has remained ready to negotiate a settlement throughout the war, though whether it is still prepared to grant France special privileges is more doubtful.

The first Vietnamese offer to negotiate after the generalization of hostilities came from Ho's mountain headquarters on April 25, 1947. Several weeks later, Professor Paul Mus, one of France's leading experts on Indo-China and then adviser to the newly appointed High Commissioner, M. Emile Bollaert, brought the French answer to Ho at a meeting some sixty miles beyond the last French outpost. France's terms for a cease fire amounted in effect to unconditional surrender. Here they are:

(1) Surrender of all arms;

(2) Complete liberty for French troops to circulate throughout Vietnam;

(3) Delivery to the French command of all non-Vietnamese combatants in the Vietnamese army;

(4) Obligatory withdrawal of Vietnamese troops to zones designated by the French command;

(5) Return of French hostages.*

Professor Mus, writing in *Le Monde* two years later, recounts how Ho Chi Minh, on hearing these terms, answered, with evident reference to the third paragraph: "In the French Union there is no place for cowards; if I accepted these conditions, I would be one."†

A check of the French press over the years of war reveals that the Vietnamese offer to negotiate a settlement was reiterated on many occasions. The following list of dates makes no claim to be exhaustive: June 14, June 20, July 18, September 23, September 30, 1947; January 15, April 12, September 6, December 21, 1948; July 20, December 20, 1949; January 2, 1950; December 25, 1951. After this, there seems to have been a relatively long interval. Then came Ho Chi Minh's famous interview with the Swedish paper *Expressen* last November in which he said: "If, drawing the lessons of these years of war, the French government wants to conclude an armistice and resolve the problem of Vietnam by negotiations, the people and the government of the Democratic Republic of Vietnam are ready to consider French proposals." But there were no French proposals forthcoming, either then or when Ho's offer was again repeated in March of this year by the Vietnamese Foreign Minister.

The French attitude of rejection and silence is quite understandable. France started the war in the first place because she thought she could win a military victory and dictate her own terms of settlement. Professor Mus, to whom we have already referred as an expert on Indo-China and an official emissary to

---

* Rivet, *op. cit.,* p. 58.
† *Ibid.,* p. 59.

the Vietnamese, has written of an interview he had with General de Gaulle, then head of the French government, in January 1946. At the end, according to the professor, de Gaulle drew himself up to his full height and said: "We shall return to Indo-China because we are the stronger."* This is precisely the attitude that has dominated French thinking all along: it precludes the very idea of negotiation.

As we write, the Indo-China phase of the Geneva conference which opened on April 26 is about to start. With Dien-bienphu lost and the whole of the Tonkin delta threatened, the French can hardly have any more illusions about being "the stronger." For the first time in seven years, official representatives of France and the Republic of Vietnam are about to sit down at the same table together. We shall soon know, perhaps even before this is in print, whether the present leaders of France have at last had a change of heart and are willing to negotiate. If they are ready, it is certain that they will not get as favorable terms as they could have had without ever firing a shot or losing a soldier. If they are not ready, it seems unlikely that they will long remain the leaders of France

The Resurrection of Bao Dai

Two days after the French in Indo-China were locked up by the Japanese on March 9, 1945, Emperor Bao Dai made a declaration before all his ministers:

The government of the Empire of Annam has today denounced the Franco-Annamite protectorate treaty and has declared the complete independence of the Empire of Annam which will henceforth strive to live as an independent nation. At the same time, as a member state of Greater East Asia it will cooperate in achieving co-existence and co-prosperity, conformably to the common declaration of Greater Asia. Therefore, the Empire of Annam declares that, to attain these goals, it will collaborate with all its strength with Japan, entrusting itself entirely to the sincerity and goodwill of the Empire of Japan.†

---

* Paul Mus, "Ma 'mission' auprès du Vietminh: ne recommençons pas 1947," *L'Observateur,* December 24, 1953, p. 24.

† Rivet, *op. cit.,* pp. 59-60.

Five months later, Bao Dai's reign ended in an act of abdication in which he declared: "We cannot repress a certain feeling of regret at the thought of our twenty years' reign during which it has been impossible for us to render any appreciable service to our country."*

Having accepted the position of "Supreme Councillor" to the new Republic of Vietnam as plain Mr. Vinh Tuy, the ex-Emperor repaired to Hong Kong, there to enjoy the fleshpots of Oriental night life and, no doubt, to make suitable contacts among the innumerable diplomats and special agents who swarm around that fantastic city.

It was there that William C. Bullitt, former United States Ambassador to Paris, self-proclaimed friend of France and enemy of Communism, found the ex-Emperor and had a heart-to-heart talk with him. Shortly after, in the month of September 1947, the French Consul in Hong Kong telegraphed M. Bollaert, French High Commissioner in Saigon: "Mr. Bullitt received from his conversation with Bao Dai a very favorable impression and was surprised at the comprehension of the ex-Emperor, with whom, he says, it is possible to reach a soltuion."† It was at this time that Bao Dai announced his acceptance of leadership of the anti-Ho Chi Minh forces in Vietnam.

The solution Mr. Bullitt had in mind was set out in an article in *Life* magazine, issue of December 22, 1947. His "recommendations" to the French government were: (1) Kick out of France the delegation of the Vietnamese Republic then resident in Paris; (2) permit the non-Communist Vietnamese nationalists to form political, economic, and military organizations for controlling the country; (3) deal with the nationalists, especially with a view to opening up military bases to them; (4) cooperate with the nationalists in crushing the Communists.

Of course, it may have been pure coincidence, but in any case the French government was already acting precisely in

---

* *Ibid.,* p. 60.

† Jacques Mitterand, "La France doit traiter," *Cahiers Internationaux,* October 1950, p. 40. At the time this article was written, Mitterand was a Councillor of the French Union.

accordance with Mr. Bullitt's advice. Five months later, on June 5, 1948, High Commissioner Bollaert signed the first of a series of accords with Bao Dai on board a French warship in the Bay of Along. By this agreement, "France solemnly recognizes the independence of Vietnam which has the privilege of freely realizing its own unity" and Vietnam "proclaims its adhesion to the French Union."*

"Hegel remarks somewhere," wrote Marx in the opening lines of *The Eighteenth Brumaire of Louis Bonaparte,* "that all great, world-historical facts and personages occur, as it were, twice. He has forgotten to add: the first time as tragedy, the second as farce. Caussidière for Danton, Louis Blanc for Robespierre, the Mountain of 1848 to 1851 for the Mountain of 1793 to 1795, the Nephew for the Uncle." Today we should add: Bao Dai for Ho Chi Minh, the "nationalists" of Hong Kong for the Vietminh.

We will not tax the reader's patience with an account of the ever renewed negotiations between the French government and Bao Dai that have taken place in the years since this first agreement. Suffice it to say that they have been, as it were, a distorted reflection of the relations between France and the Vietnamese armies on the battlefields of Indo-China. Had France been able to win military victories, Bao Dai would have settled for anything he could get. But as France steadily lost ground to Ho Chi Minh's armies, Bao Dai's bargaining power rose until in the latest agreements it appears that France has been forced to concede, at least on paper, a considerably greater degree of independence than it has fought eight years to withhold from the Ho Chi Minh regime. Another illustration of history's fondness for irony. . . .

Bao Dai's re-entry onto the stage was no solo performance. From the first conversations with Mr. Bullitt, the former Emperor, now transformed into a "Chief of State," was accompanied and prompted by official and unofficial representatives of the United States. A steady stream of American notables—

---

* Rivet, *op. cit.,* p. 61.

businessmen, cardinals and monsignori,* political VIPs from Governor Dewey to Vice President Nixon—has moved into and around the French-controlled areas of Indo-China. And this stream has been matched by other streams—of dollars to France and arms to Saigon and Haiphong.

In a strictly military sense, the war in Indo-China is still France's war. But in every other sense it has become America's war. Bao Dai, like the Bidaults and Pinays and Laniels who thought to use him, is Washington's man: his growing independence of France is but a measure of his growing dependence on the United States.

The situation, of course, is an untenable one. France cannot and will not go on bleeding for others. The reasons for this are not only and perhaps not even mainly political. They are also military: continuation of the war in Indo-China on the present basis would inevitably lead to the demoralization of the French officer corps. Here are the conclusions on this subject reached by Claude Bourdet and his fellow editors of *France-Observateur* after painstaking questioning of higher French officers who know the Indo-China situation well:

Up to now the morale of French officers has remained high. Disasters like that at Hoa-Binh which also [that is, as in the case of Dienbienphu] resulted from a political masquerade made an unfavorable impression on them; but the French army has a tradition of not discussing overall plans no matter whether they succeed or fail. Even Dienbienphu would perhaps not have affected them deeply [this was written a week before the fall of Dienbienphu]. But it is precisely because these officers could assent to such heavy sacrifices in so questionable a war on the simple ground that

---

* There are some two million Roman Catholics in Indo-China, including Bao Dai's wife, the ex-Empress Nam Phuong. In 1948, Cardinal Spellman and Msgr. Fulton Sheen visited the country—for reasons which were well expressed in a sermon which Sheen delivered in the Saigon Cathedral. "We bring to the peoples of Indo-China," he said, "the greetings of the Roman Catholic Church which has the greatest solicitude for the children of the Far East. Old Europe is politically finished. The Catholic Church is counting greatly on the Far East which will become a solid pillar of the faith of Christ in a hundred or two hundred years. . . . The Far Eastern visit of Cardinal Spellman is the best proof of the Roman Catholic Church's interest in the Far East." Quoted from French Catholic sources by Rivet, *op. cit.*, pp. 61-62.

"the interest of France demands it"—it is precisely for this reason that they are so revolted by the idea of fighting for Bao Dai who is distrusted by them as much as he is by his compatriots. It's no good reasoning and invoking the "solidarity of the free world"; one can no longer prevent the French officers from feeling that they are fighting for Maximilian [the ill-fated French invader of Mexico in the 1860's]: the state of mind of those returning to France or writing home is changing from day to day.*

But the morale of the officer corps is by no means the only military problem facing France as a result of the Indo-Chinese war. What is at stake is really nothing more nor less than the destruction of the French army as an effective fighting force. Here are a few extremely revealing excerpts from an article entitled "To Save the French Army" which appeared in *Le Monde* of April 29th under the signature of Robert Guillain, a special correspondent very recently back from Indo-China:

I can still hear a friend in Indo-China saying to me as I was about to return: "Tell them that the hour of truth has struck. It is your duty to speak out." It was a military man speaking. I adjure my readers not to think that I am propagating defeatism. I affirm that I am speaking in the name of a great number of our soldiers and officers, men whose patriotism is beyond question, when I repeat what they have told me and what I have again and again been able to verify myself: the continuation of the war in Indo-China will mean the loss of our army [*met notre armé en perdition*].

It is an army decimated, full of gaps, exhausted. The terrible fault of our governors has been to demand without cease the performance of a task too big and at the same time to refuse the means of carrying it out. When an army has a mission beyond its means, the only possible course, if one does not want to see this army destroy itself, is to reduce the mission to the means available. But it is just the opposite that is being contemplated: the mission is to be kept and as a result it will be necessary to throw into the war everything that is left of our army in France, in Europe, and in the French Union.

The chief result of this war, fought with means insufficient to the tasks assigned, is that the command, at both Paris and Saigon, has had to look on in anguish while its cadres were disappearing in the crucible. The French army is not building itself up today, it is destroying itself. Judge for yourself.

---

* "Vietnam: L'Armée dégage sa responsabilité," *France-Observateur* (formerly *L'Observateur*), April 29, 1954, p. 9.

Today we are not replacing officers as fast as they are being destroyed. It is now three graduating classes from Saint Cyr [France's West Point] that will have been destroyed in the last two years.

Since the beginning of this year, 1954, the number of French officers killed comes to about 250. If this pace continues we shall have lost by the end of the year 800 officers. The war in Indo-China is cutting our ranks on a scale comparable to a great international war.

The treacherous war in the Tonkin Delta, the least known and nevertheless the most terrible, sees on the average one officer fall every day. Thirty every month. Three hundred and sixty every year.

How replace all those who fall? It is here that there arises with dramatic intensity the problem of the "third tour of duty" and even of the "fourth tour of duty." A large number of our officers have been in Indo-China four or even six years. How can we demand of them that they serve another tour? How continue to insure replacements? And are we not witnessing the aging of our cadres, a striking deterioration of their quality, not to mention that of the simple recruits which becomes more and more disturbing?

There are, of course, no answers to these heart-rending questions. The French army is at the end of its resources. Faced with this fact, even the most intransigent rightist must call a halt. It is clear now that either the war must be stopped or it must become wholly America's war. Bao Dai's second reign is about to come to an inglorious end, or else this "Chief of State" (whom President Eisenhower addressed as "Your Majesty" after the fall of Dienbienphu) is about to take his place alongside Syngman Rhee and Chiang Kai-shek in Washington's stable of "Asian fighters against Asians."

The Legitimate Government of Vietnam

American government spokesmen and the American press are all but unanimous in telling us that the Bao Dai outfit is the legitimate government of Vietnam, and that the regime which Ho Chi Minh heads is merely "the Vietminh rebels." This interpretation is presumably based on the following facts: In March 1949, Bao Dai exchanged letters with President Vincent Auriol of France which, when ratified, would make Vietnam an "Associated State." A similar procedure was carried out between France on the one hand and Laos and Cambodia on the other. Thus, by the end of 1949 these three regimes were, by French fiat as it were, declared to be "independent sovereign states," and they were promptly recognized as such by the Western powers.

A fine piece of political alchemy, surely. But it has one weakness: it failed to dispose of the Democratic Republic of Vietnam which, by all rules and canons of international law, was and is the legitimate government of Vietnam. On this point, let us hear the authoritative opinion of the French expert Gérard Lyon-Caen, Professor of Law at the University of Dijon:

Which of the two governments, that of the Republic or that of the ex-Emperor Bao Dai, is the legitimate government of Vietnam?

As a matter of law, the question is not open to doubt, *the only legitimate government is that of the Vietnamese Republic,* and this for two sets of reasons:

(1) After his abdication of 1945, Bao Dai, according to his own statements, was nothing but a plain citizen. He was without any mandate to treat on behalf of his country with the French, a fact which renders the Auriol-Bao Dai accords of no juridical value and precludes their binding the Vietnamese nation. In addition, the government which he established did not result from regular democratic elections. To be recognized as a government the first condition is to be a *de facto* government, a government exercising effective authority over the majority of its territory and citizens: that is not true of Bao Dai's government which can come and go only where it is accompanied by French bayonets, that is to say, in a few centers.

(2) On the other hand, the government formed by President Ho Chi Minh has authority over the greater part of the country and enjoys the confidence of its inhabitants. In January 1946—an unprecedented event—there took place elections in all Vietnam, general elections with universal suffrage from which emerged the present National Assembly. The latter is therefore the sole depositary of national sovereignty, and the government of Vietnam is that which enjoys the confidence of this Assembly. Since August 1945 there has been no interruption in the exercise of power, and the government of the Republic conserves the legitimacy which the

French government itself conceded to it when it signed with it the accords of March 6, 1946.*

This might seem to be a quibble about unimportant legal technicalities. Actually it is much more. It is decisive for the whole question of who is guilty of aggression in Indo-China. No country is entitled, legally or morally, to set up the private citizen of another country as a government and to support that "government" with its armed forces. This is what the Soviet Union did in the case of Finland in 1939, and the Western powers were, quite rightly, unanimous in condemning the action. Subsequently the Soviet Union made at least partial amends by dropping the Kuusinen "government" and dealing once again with the legitimate Finnish government. France has done exactly the same thing in Vietnam, but the Western powers, far from condemning the action, have put their stamp of approval on it by recognizing the Bao Dai puppet regime. France, needless to say, has still to make amends.

Legally, there is not the slightest doubt that the French are guilty of aggression in Indo-China, nor that France's allies are fully implicated as knowing aids and accomplices. No amount of screaming about the "aggression" of "Communist imperialism," an entity with no existence in international law, can hide this damning fact from anyone who will take the trouble to examine the record of what has happened in Indo-China in the last eight years.

Communism and Indo-China

This is not to say that Communism, national and international, is not playing an important role in Indo-China, or that the facts in this regard are not a matter of perfectly legitimate concern to outsiders. The question is what *are* the facts?

First, as to Ho Chi Minh. Perhaps as good a brief biography as any is that given by Professor Rivet of Paris:

Ho Chi Minh is a Tonkinese peasant, a "ñakue." His life has been one of poverty and struggle. He is a Marxist. In 1914 he

---

* Gérard Lyon-Caen, "La République démocratique du Vietnam," *Cahiers Internationaux*, October 1950. It should perhaps be added that no change has taken place in the legal position since 1950.

joined the French Socialist Party to which he belonged until the split of Tours (1920). Many of our Socialist leaders and militants knew him, living meagerly from his trade as a photographer. At the time of the split, he went with the majority and joined the Third International. Persecuted in Indo-China, he fled to Russia where he lived in as great poverty as he had in France until, along about 1926, he was made a professor at a popular Indo-Chinese university established at Canton.

Ho Chi Minh knows our country [France], Russia, and China. He speaks French fluently. Returning to Indo-China in 1940, he became leader of the Resistance and of the party of Vietnamese independence, and in due course the confidence of his countrymen elevated him to the first place in the country. Ho Chi Minh is a Communist and has never hidden the fact, but he is above all a patriot. He is a scrupulously honest man and lives the life of an ascetic.*

From the same set of facts, Mr. John Foster Dulles paints the following portrait of Ho Chi Minh: "He was indoctrinated in Moscow. He became an associate of the Russian, Borodin, when the latter was organizing the Chinese Communist Party which was to bring China into the Soviet orbit. Then Ho transferred his activities to Indo-China." (Speech of March 29.) No comment seems necessary—except maybe that Borodin did not arrive in China until well after the organization of the Chinese Communist Party, and the major achievement with which historians credit him is the reorganization not of the Communist Party but of the Kuomintang.

What do the Vietnamese think of Ho? On this subject, all knowledgeable observers seem to be in agreement: he is held in the highest esteem, an esteem approaching reverence, by all his people. We will be content with a quotation from one among many sources by no means sympathetic to the Republic or Communism which might be cited. Writes Peggy Durdin in the New York Times Magazine of May 9th:

Through more than seven bitter war years his name has been an asset beyond price to the Vietminh. What the simple peasants might not have done or suffered for an abstraction called communism—or even for that other abstraction called national independence—they have done and suffered for "Uncle Ho." . . . Nor

* Rivet, op. cit., p. 46.

is the veneration for Ho confined to the Vietminh side. Many Vietnamese who would willingly work against China-aided communism are reluctant to take a stand against Ho Chi Minh. Most Vietnamese believe that it is Ho Chi Minh who has wrenched from the French whatever degree of independence Bao Dai's Vietnam has achieved. "He is so greatly revered even on this side," said one official of the Bao Dai government, "that we don't dare attack him in our propaganda. . . ." "They have Ho Chi Minh and we have nothing," says a French officer bitterly (p. 12 and pp. 69-71).

Turning now to the part played by the Communist Party in the Democratic Republic of Vietnam, there is little room for doubt as to the facts here either. The regime is a coalition of all patriotic organizations and groups—political, religious, and occupational—but the leading positions are held by Communists. Joseph Starobin, a correspondent for the *Daily Worker* who visited liberated Vietnam in 1953, has described the political situation simply and frankly in his informative book, *Eyewitness in Indo-China,* which has just been published:

There is no question that the Lao Dong [Communist Party] is the leading force. It is the party that provides the backbone of the government. But it is also true that the Lao Dong has known how to rally around itself a wide variety of other political circles. This ability is surely one of the secrets of its success (p. 122).

But the chief secret of its success, naturally, has been its effectiveness in providing leadership under extremely difficult conditions. Starting virtually from scratch, the Republic has built up an administration, an army, a by no means negligible manufacturing industry, an educational system; and it has done all this while fighting an all-out war and without controlling the urban nerve centers of the economy. The achievement is fully comparable to that of the Chinese Revolution, and the Communists have played a similarly distinguished and important role in the two countries.

Which raises the question of the role of the Chinese and Chinese Communism in Indo-China. Needless to say, this role was nonexistent, or at most negligible, prior to 1950. It was not until then that the Chinese liberation armies reached the Indo-Chinese border and established regular contact with the Ho Chi Minh government. By that time, the Republic had passed through its darkest days, and its armies had already begun the process of compressing and winning back the regions under French control. Soon afterwards, the Korean War broke out and absorbed all available Chinese military supplies and energies. There was trade, certainly involving arms already located in the South of China, across the Tonkin-Yunnan border; some Vietnamese personnel probably went to China for specialized training in this period. But no one, so far as we are aware, claims that Chinese assistance was a decisive factor for the Republic, either economically or militarily, while the Korean War was still in progress.

Things are supposed to have changed after the Korean Armistice. And doubtless they did. The Chinese and other countries in the socialist bloc had long since recognized the Republican regime as the legitimate government of Vietnam—an action which, in accordance with what we have learned, was perfectly legal and proper—and it would be surprising indeed if they did not expand their economic relations as soon and as fast as conditions would permit. The Vietnamese undoubtedly purchase as much arms and munitions as they can pay for and transport, and it is important to understand that this is a growing amount which has been a decisive factor in enabling the Republican army to adopt the new strategy and tactics which won the battle of Dienbienphu. It is also important to understand that the flow of arms and munitions from China to the Republic has never been and, for purely physical reasons connected with the scarcity of railroads and good roads, can hardly be expected to be in the foreseeable future anything like as large as the stream of arms and munitions from the United States to the French and the Bao Dai forces.

Furnishing arms, munitions, and even technical aid is one thing; furnishing combat manpower is another. It is the latter which the United States has been constantly threatening to do since Dulles' speech to the Overseas Press Club on March 29th. The excuse is that China is already furnishing fighting forces to the Vietnamese. In his April 5th appearance before the House Foreign Affairs Committee, Dulles presented an intelligence document which, according to the *New York Times* of the next day, had "presumably just been cleared through this country's highest strategic body, the National Security Council," and which Dulles said "told an ominous story." Here is the document as presented in the *Times:*

Most recent advices with respect to extent of Communist Chinese participation in the fighting at Dienbienphu indicate the following:

1. A Chinese Communist general, Li Chen-hou, is stationed at the Dienbienphu headquarters of General Giap, the Vietminh commander.

2. Under him there are nearly a score of Chinese Communist technical military advisers at headquarters of General Giap. Also, there are numerous other Chinese Communists military advisers at division level.

3. There are special telephone lines installed, maintained and operated by Chinese personnel.

4. There are a considerable number of .37-mm anti-aircraft guns radar-controlled at Dienbienphu, which are shooting through the clouds to bring ddwn French aircraft. These guns are operated by Chinese.

5. In support of the battle there are approximately 1,000 supply trucks of which about one-half have arrived since March 1, all driven by Chinese Army personnel.

6. All the foregoing is, of course, in addition to the fact that the artillery, the ammunition and equipment generally comes from Communist China.

At the time, it was of course quite impossible for an outsider to evaluate these claims. But since then we have had some strong and pointed statements from the French who are in a much better position than Mr. Dulles to know the real situation in Indo-China. They permit us to say with reasonable assurance either that Mr. Dulles was grossly imposed upon (by his brother in the Central Intelligence Agency perhaps?) or that he is guilty of propagating a deliberate falsehood. In either case it is unpleasant, to say the least, to think that we may some day go to war on the strength of an intelligence report.

Charles Favrel, correspondent for *Le Monde,* tells in a dispatch from Hanoi, dated merely "April" and published on the 22nd of that month, of an airplane trip to Dienbienphu to parachute matériel to the beleaguered garrison. His purpose in going along, he tells us at the outset, was "to try to discover the characteristic cranium of one of those Chinese whom Messrs. Dulles and Laniel, from the vantage points of Washington and Paris, have perceived in the Vietminh army."

M. Favrel's first surprise was the accuracy of the AA fire which from the first shot came within a few meters of the plane. His second was to discover that incoming French pilots and ground communicated with each other *in the clear* about all details of position, cargoes to be dropped, and so on. Let M. Favrel take up the story at this point:

If you were to furnish such data of a problem to the stupidest examinee, he would ask if you were making fun of him and would keep his fingers crossed, expecting a trap!

The Viet gunners, whose ears are on their heads, do not try to understand: they shoot. No need of radar for this cut-and-dried job! Better still, the V.H.F. [Very High Frequency] gives them all details about the cargoes so that no one need be in ignorance. It says:

"*Ici Gros-Matou, cap 305*. Altitude 9,500 feet at ten minutes from the vertical. Mission parachuting mortar shells.

"*Ici Bolero, cap 300*. Altitude 9,000 feet at seventeen minutes from the vertical. Mission napalm on Dominique 7."

And the aviation Command Post for directing the various planes according to urgency and priority:

"*Pour Gros-Matou,* you will veer left thirty seconds after the top to come at 7,000 feet onto the axis of the dropping zone.

"*Pour Bolero,* go up to 10,000 feet and wait in the eastern sector."*

The Viet gunners who are given the coordinates for their fire have all the time for preparation. But still there are at our staff headquarters innocent souls who are astonished that reinforcements parachuted in at night are regularly met on the ground by flares specially prepared for them!

The question arises as to who first started circulating the story of the radar-controlled guns? I don't know who he was but I know his colleague who first put over the American airwaves the fable of the flying saucers in the air over Dienbienphu!

In this respect it is disturbing to have to state that the censorship which puts all sorts of obstacles in the way of our transmission of correct news, complacently passes the delirious inventions

---

* Our command of military French is shaky to say the least but hardly so inadequate as to obscure the point.

which the specialists in sensationalism discover in the resources of their imaginations.

Mr. Foster Dulles himself has taken up and put the stamp of his approval on the best of their finds. Only there is a little catch: on March 28th the Bigeard counter-attack on the village of Ban-Ong-Pet enabled us to capture five AA guns—guns which had no radar.

But Mr. Dulles, who has a poor opinion of the Viet gunners, sticks to his Chinese. He has disposed them on the battlefield and, having qualified them as radar operators, telephone specialists, truck drivers, technical advisers, etc., he endows them with a general, a certain Ly Chen-hou whose name he discovered in the gallery of faded stars to which were relegated the glories of Chiang Kai-shek's army which occupied Indo-China north of the 16th parallel.

The misfortune is that the Second Bureau [military intelligence] of the Tonkin Zone, which is in a better position than the Pentagon to know what is going on on the spot, has formally denied such allegations.

That the Vietminh cadres are formed in China, agreed. That food comes from China is certain. That some Russian and Czech matériel has been brought in is proved. But neither interrogations of prisoners of war nor the information furnished by our agents has given evidence of a single Chinese in the Vietminh armies.

And if certain official commentaries emanating from Saigon have emboldened M. Laniel to come to the assistance of Mr. Foster Dulles, these commentaries have been fabricated to meet the needs of the case.

If there is any desire to undertake an inquiry into the manner in which propaganda which flies in the face of realities is organized, there still are, fortunately, honest officers and generals who will say what they think of the business.

To this story, so revealing of the way of both soldiers and statesmen, we may add the finding of the editors of *France-Observateur* on the basis of careful inquiry in military circles in Paris:

There are no Chinese on the Vietminh side except possibly some technical advisers *who do not fight* and perhaps some drivers of automobiles. At one time it was thought that the AA was manned by Chinese. This hypothesis has been given up. It has been noted that the Russian instructions for using the AA guns have been translated into Vietnamese, and there is no indication of the presence of Chinese personnel. On the contrary, on the occasion of the Bigeard parachutist counter-offensive in March, five AA pieces were captured by the French, their crews killed or captured. There were only Vietnamese among them.*

So much, then, for Dulles' charges of Chinese participation in the Republican army. They were obviously made up out of whole cloth for the purpose of deceiving the American people and preparing them for a more direct role in the Indo-Chinese war.

To sum up the problem of Communism and Indo-China: Ho Chi Minh is a Communist and a patriot who is held in the highest esteem by the entire Vietnamese nation. The Communists have come to occupy the leading role in the Democratic Republic of Vietnam, not by the devious methods of conspiracy nor by appointment of Peking or Moscow, but because they proved themselves capable of providing effective leadership under the extremely difficult conditions of a war for national independence from colonial oppression. The aid they have received from the Chinese and Russians has not exceeded what is perfectly legal and proper for the government of one country to furnish to that of another.

You may not like Communism—that is everyone's right—but you cannot honestly talk about freedom and at the same time deny the right of the Vietnamese to choose Communist leadership if they want it, as they apparently do. And it is the sheerest kind of hypocrisy to assert that China does not have the right to do for the legitimate Democratic Republic of Vietnam what the United States claims the right to do on a much larger scale for France and the illegitimate regime of Bao Dai.

Which Way America?

The American people, by and large, are against colonialism and aggression and believe in the right of every country to manage its own affairs free from outside interference.

Rarely have these simple principles been so clearly and grossly violated as in present United States policy toward Indo-China.

---

* "Vietnam: L'armée dégage sa responsabilité," *France-Observateur,* April 29, 1954, p. 9.

To the extent that we support France—and we are already paying about four-fifths of the cost of the French military effort in Indochina—we support both colonialism and aggression. To the extent that we support Bao Dai, we claim the right to tell the Vietnamese people who should rule them. And if we send American forces into Indo-China, as Dulles and other high government spokesmen have repeatedly threatened to do in the last two months, we shall be guilty of aggression ourselves.

There is no way to avoid these conclusions about our policy and no extenuating circumstances to excuse it. The facts, as we hope the foregoing recital has shown to the satisfaction of even the most skeptical, are clear and unambiguous.

What are we going to do about it?

Are we going to take the position that anti-Communism justifies anything, including colonialism, interference in the affairs of other countries, and aggression? That way, let us be perfectly clear about it, lies war and more war leading ultimately to full-scale national disaster.

Or are we going to call a halt to the degrading and ruinous policy our leaders have been pursuing and begin to find our way back to a course based on the principles on which this country was founded, the principles of national independence and respect for the rights of others?

There never has been and never will be a clearer test case than Indo-China. The time for decision is now. Let everyone who cares about the future of our country stand up and speak out today. Tomorrow may be too late.

The Approaching Crisis

Through the fog of censorship and official double talk, it is becoming possible to see more and more clearly the approach of an historically momentous crisis in Vietnam.

Washington's cynical discarding of the Diem-Nhu regime of course solved nothing. The new military junta may be more pliable and readier to do Washington's bidding. For a few weeks, the people of South Vietnam, out of a sense of relief to be rid of the old tyrants, may have half hoped that things would really change for the better. But the American policy of "getting on with the business of killing Communists" never promised anything but more misery and bitterness; and hopes for the new regime, which is new only in the sense that there has taken place a change in personnel at the top, were bound to be short lived. It is now clear that the demise of Diem and Nhu, far from marking the opening of a new chapter, was simply a signal that the old chapter was coming to an end.

After a brief lull, the Vietcong—which of course includes not only Communists but representatives of all patriotic elements in the country—has stepped up the scope and intensity of the guerrilla war. News filtering through the censorship permits us to assume that the situation of the government in the Mekong River Delta, always a stronghold of the rebels, has become desperate. But there have also been, for the first time in a long while, reports of severe government defeats and losses in the provinces to the north of Saigon. And now comes news that the rising rebel tide is threatening to inundate Saigon itself. In an important dispatch to the *New York Times*, Hedrick Smith describes the situation in the capital in the following somber terms:

The conflict is no further away at times than Westchester County is from New York City.

Late last month, 300 guerrillas stole into a heavily armed camp 20 miles west of Saigon. They inflicted heavy casualties and made off with loads of arms, money, and ammunition. From Saigon roofs, the deep boom of the government's artillery could be heard. And on clear days patrons lunching in the ninth-floor restaurant of the Caravelle Hotel can watch government planes dropping napalm on guerrillas across the Saigon River.

From almost every direction, guerrillas creep close to Saigon and their attacks grow bolder. "They've drawn a collar right around the city," one United States military spokesman said. (*New York Times,* Western edition, December 7, 1963.)

Even without detailed or inside information, one can feel reasonably certain that this upsurge of rebel activity and power is no flash in the pan but rather arises directly out of the constellation of forces created by the fall of the Diem-Nhu regime. Prior to the October coup, it was possible for many South Vietnamese who still did not see matters clearly to blame the sorry plight of their country on an obviously corrupt, brutal, and tyrannical clique at the head of the government. But now that this clique, or at least its leading figures, have been liquidated, can one assume that the people will simply transfer the same attitudes to the new clique and look for salvation from a new coup and more liquidations? Having seen that the operation failed the first time to produce any improvement, are they likely to entertain hope that a repetition could produce better results?

The answers seem obvious. Crying wolf yields rapidly diminishing returns, and so does overthrowing regimes which differ from each other only in names and faces. This might make little difference if there were no alternatives. The history of many Latin American countries, for example, has been one long succession of regimes, one as bad as or worse than the other. The people have long since grown cynical, discounting the talk of their oppressors at a full 100 percent and expecting nothing but more of the same. But that was because they neither saw nor could imagine an alternative.

The situation in Vietnam is radically different. There, there is an alternative—the National Liberation Front and its military arm, the Vietcong, which have been waging *and winning* a prolonged political and military struggle under the most

difficult conditions and against the greatest odds. Disillusion-
ed by the post-Diem junta, the long-suffering and embittered
people of South Vietnam can hardly help turning their eyes
and thoughts to the guerrillas who now become their only
hope for peace and a better life.

If this is correct, it accounts for two kinds of reactions.
Many who have hitherto wavered in indecision or even hoped
for improvement within the present framework, go over to
the rebels. And many who for one reason or another are not in
a position to join the rebels stop supporting or start sabotaging
the government. Both reactions to the new political situation
alter the balance of forces in favor of the rebels and against
the government; together they may explain the dramatic change
in the military situation which has come about in the last
few weeks.

At this distance, it is of course quite impossible to predict
the timetable of events from here on. But the direction in which
they are moving seems irreversible. And if due account be
taken of likely bandwagon and snowball effects, the possibility
that matters will now move rapidly to a head must be taken
seriously. One is reminded of the final months of struggle
against Batista in Cuba when the masses moved decisively into
the rebel ranks and even the tyrant's heavily armed troops
melted away. Once in sight, the end came quickly.

The denouement in Vietnam, however, cannot be the
same as it was in Cuba. In the Cuban arena there were only
two parties involved, the rebels and the government. In the
Vietnamese arena, there are three—the Vietcong, the government, and the United States. If the government collapses, as
Batista's did, the Vietcong will not be able simply to take over,
as the Fidelistas did: it will still be facing the United States,
with thousands of its own soldiers already on the ground and
tens of thousands ready to be airlifted in, quite literally on a
moment's notice.

It is this prospective confrontation which constitutes the
heart and core of the historic crisis which we can now see shaping
up in Vietnam. And the outcome, as in the case of earlier postwar crises in the Far East, will depend essentially on United
States policy.

Washington will have to decide between two radically different courses of action: either establish United States military rule in South Vietnam and assume full responsibility for conduct of the war, or make peace. It is important that we should try, now rather than later, to understand the implications of these fundamental alternatives.

As long as the war is being conducted by a South Vietnamese government, its objective, however unattainable, is unambiguously defined: to liquidate the guerrillas and restore law and order. In these circumstances, the United States appears in the guise of a friend and helper, trying to do for the local government what the Soviet Union did for the Kadar government in Hungary in 1956. But if the local government collapses, what will the role of the United States then be? Can it continue to pursue the same war aims?

The answer is that the United States would then assume the posture of a military occupier, and the purpose of continuing the war as a strictly South Vietnamese affair could only be the maintenance of an out-and-out military colony on the Asian mainland. Let us be perfectly clear about one thing: in the world of today, this would not be a tenable position for the United States to be in. No country can fight a war to maintain its own control over foreign territory to which it has not the shadow of a legal or historic claim. In order to justify continuation of the war, new and broader aims would have to be espoused and the character of the war would have to be correspondingly changed.

There is no mystery about what the new war aims would be: to unify Vietnam and cut out the alleged roots of the "subversive" forces which make impossible a solution of the problem within the confines of South Vietnam. What we wrote of the Korean War, commemorating the first anniversary of its outbreak more than twelve years ago, applies with full force and effect to the Vietnamese war today:

This was a case in which . . . it was either necessary to go forward or to pull back. The Korean War had a logic of its own which asserted itself regardless of the will of the individuals who seemed to be running it: either it had to be expanded or it had to be stopped ("Korea—One Year Later," *Monthly Review*, August 1951, p. 116.)

In the case of the Korean War, it *was* expanded—once. That was when MacArthur, with Truman's acquiescence, crossed the 38th parallel and carried the war to North Korea. But when MacArthur, representing powerful forces in the United States and desperate men like Rhee and Chiang in Asia, attempted the second expansion into China itself, Truman pulled back. Again the logic of the war asserted itself, albeit agonizingly and bloodily: it was finally stopped by Truman's successor.

The great question in Vietnam now is whether this process must be repeated. Are American forces, stymied in South Vietnam, going to flee forward into North Vietnam? If they do, China will of course come to the aid of her ally, and the fateful question of the second expansion will be ineluctably posed. In Korea, the decision was for peace; but those who are old enough to remember the frightful months of December and January in the winter of 1950-1951 and the "MacArthur crisis" which followed, know how close the balance was, how perilously the world trembled on the brink of disaster. Must we go through this again, with no assurance whatever that the decision would this time be in favor of the survival of the human race?

The alternative, of course, is to make peace in Vietnam. It can be done on honorable terms and without loss of face by anyone. What is required is simply that the terms of the Geneva Agreement of 1954 should be honestly observed. Immediately after the Geneva Conference, we wrote:

The Geneva settlement of the Indo-China War was a genuine compromise which, assuming good will and good sense on both sides, can bring great benefits to everyone concerned. This is obvious enough as far as the Vietnamese are concerned. Not only do they get peace after eight years of the cruelest kind of war; in addition, they are promised the unity of their country in terms which it would be hard for the French to circumvent even if they should be so foolish as to try. ("The Consequences of Geneva," *Monthly Review,* September 1954, p. 161.)

Let it be said to the credit of the French that they were not so foolish as to try; that ignominious role was assumed by the United States. Now, after nine more years of the cruelest kind of war, the foolishness of the effort has been fully demonstrated in the eyes of the whole world. Is it not time to admit it, honestly and frankly, and to return to the ways of negotiation and compromise?

We do not mean to suggest that the Geneva Agreement of 1954 is fully suited, in all its details, to the present situation. Much has changed in the past nine years, and doubtless a new and more appropriate instrument could be devised. If this is so, then what is needed is evidently a new Geneva Conference to bring the labors of the old one up to date. But the underlying principles of the old agreement are as valid today as they were nine years ago. They are, put in their simplest terms, self-determination for the Vietnamese people and international guarantees of the inviolability of Vietnamese territory.

The Road to Ruin

> *I am sure that the great American people, if they only knew the true facts and the background to the developments in South Vietnam, will agree with me that further bloodshed is unnecessary. . . . As you know, in times of war and hostilities the first casualty is truth.*
> —U Thant

The State Department's White Paper on Vietnam, released to the press on February 27th, is based entirely on one assumption, though it is not stated as such but is rather taken for granted as an obvious fact. The assumption is that there is a "legitimate government" (the term recurs again and again) in South Vietnam. This government is said to be trying to defend itself, and all the United States is doing is lending it needed assistance. If you accept this, you can hardly avoid the conclusion that North Vietnam is indeed guilty of aggression, though the scale is modest even on the showing of the White Paper itself. If you do not accept the idea that there is a legitimate government in South Vietnam, then the entire argument of the White Paper collapses and the facts which it adduces (assuming them all to be genuine) can only be interpreted as evidence of the remarkable caution and restraint of Hanoi in combatting a foreign occupier of a large part of Vietnamese territory.

Which is it? Is the Saigon regime a "legitimate government"? Or is it a Quisling-type puppet of a foreign occupier? Evidently our whole attitude toward the war in Vietnam must depend on how we answer these questions.

The Origin and Nature of the Saigon Regime

In seeking answers we must recall some well established facts of recent history.*

During the Second World War the French colonial regime in Indo-China collaborated with the Japanese just as the Vichy regime in France did with the Germans. Toward the end of the war, the Japanese, getting wind of a French plot to turn on them, locked up the colonial troops and administrators and set up an "independent" puppet state under the Annamite Emperor Bao Dai. Meanwhile, a resistance movement called the Vietminh, led by Ho Chi Minh and supported by the Allies (particularly by the Americans through the Office of Strategic Services), established itself in the northern part of the country and gained control over a large part of the countryside in the remainder. When the Japanese surrendered, their forces in Vietnam simply handed over power to the Vietminh which proclaimed an independent republic. That rarest of events, a peaceful transfer of power from one regime to another, took place. If the great powers had recognized the new Republic of Vietnam, there would in all probability never have been a war in that part of the world and a strong unified state would long since have come into being as a stabilizing force in the whole region of Southeast Asia. But to expect anything like that while imperialism still exists would undoubtedly be the sheerest of utopias.

At the Potsdam Conference in the summer of 1945, it was decided that Japanese forces would be disarmed and repatriated by the Chinese in the part of Vietnam north of the 17th parallel and by the British in the southern half. Chiang Kai-shek, in a complicated political maneuver, pushed a provincial Yunnanese army in from China, and the British landed forces in the South. The Yunnanese grabbed as much as they could get

---

*For the sake of brevity we do not encumber the text with numerous quotations and citations. Any reader who is interested in checking our facts and interpretations will find ample material in the following (and the sources cited therein): *The War in Vietnam,* by Hugh Deane, Monthly Review Pamphlet Series No. 23, 1963; Helen B. Lamb, *The Tragedy of Vietnam,* Basic Pamphlets, 1964; Edgar Snow, *The Other Side of the River,* New York, 1961, Chapter 85; and "What Every American Should Know About Indo-China," MONTHLY REVIEW, June 1954.

their hands on but made no attempt to interfere with the Vietnamese government, which proceeded to entrench itself in power in the North. The British on the other hand, acting on the absurd pretense that Ho Chi Minh was a puppet of the Japanese, refused to recognize the government, disarmed its troops wherever possible, and promptly brought the French back. What now happened constitutes one of the most sordid chapters in the whole shameful history of imperialist conquest; it also throws most valuable light on the question of the legitimacy of all subsequent Vietnamese regimes.

The French never had any intention of renouncing their prewar position as colonial overlords. In order to re-establish it, however, they had to cope with the reality of a Vietnamese government controlling half the country and enjoying massive popular support in the rest. They chose the methods of guile, deception, and ultimately brute force.

For the French the crux of the matter was to get their armies into the North to replace the Chinese, and to this end they undertook simultaneous negotiations in Chungking and Hanoi. The Chinese were in effect bought off, and the Vietnamese were won over by what on the face of it appeared to be an enormous concession to the Vietnamese. The agreement signed by the two governments, dated March 6, 1946, stated in its first article: "The government of France recognizes the Republic of Vietnam as a free state having its government and its parliament, its army and its finances, forming part of the Indo-Chinese federation and of the French Union." The French Union had not then been defined, but the language leaves no doubt that a status for Vietnam comparable to that of a member of the British Commonwealth was envisaged. *Legally speaking, the March 6th agreement put the stamp of legitimacy on the regime of Ho Chi Minh as the government of all Vietnam, and nothing that has happened since has changed the situation in this respect by one iota.*

The French did not intend to respect the agreement. They set about at once to subvert it, either by reducing Ho to the status of a puppet or, if that should prove impossible, by completely crushing and liquidating his regime. "We shall return to Indo-China because we are the stronger," said the head

of the French government to an interlocutor in January 1946.
His name was Charles de Gaulle, and it took him and his successors eight long years to discover that he was wrong: France
was not the stronger.

It was during these years of bitter warfare that the present
Saigon government was conceived and born. It was illegitimate
from the outset, and neither subsequent adoption by the Americans nor attempts to give it a new pedigree can disguise its continued illegitimacy.

Having failed to puppetize Ho Chi Minh, the French
were in a quandary. Naked colonial rule could obviously not
be reimposed on a people who had so recently fought for and
won genuine independence. So the French had to devise a solution which at least appeared to respect the independence of
Vietnam. For this they reached into the fleshpots of Hong Kong
and dredged up the former Emperor Bao Dai, installing him
as "Chief of State" and concluding with him an agreement
(June 5, 1948) according to which "France solemnly recognizes the independence of Vietnam which has the privilege of
freely realizing its own unity."

Does Bao Dai's return perhaps provide the basis for a
legal argument in favor of his government's legitimacy? Not at
all. After the surrender of the Japanese in 1945, Bao Dai had
voluntarily abdicated his throne, resumed his civilian name of
Vinh Tuy, and accepted the honorary position of "Supreme
Councillor" to the new Republic of Vietnam—and then de-
parted to enjoy the pleasures of Hong Kong night life. The
notion that all this could be undone and Bao Dai turned into
a legitimate ruler by French fiat is too absurd to be taken
seriously.

The Americans apparently understood this, for when they
replaced the French as the real power behind the Saigon regime
they either acquiesced in or instigated a maneuver designed to
give it a "new look." Ngo Dinh Diem had intrigued for position in the Japanese-supported Bao Dai government. But for
various reasons he failed to achieve a top post and instead went
into exile in the United States where he established solid contacts in high political circles. Back in office as "Chief of State"
after 1948 and increasingly dependent on United States hand-

outs, Bao Dai found it expedient to appoint Ngo Dinh Diem as his prime minister. At the time of the Geneva Agreements (July 1954) which marked the surrender of the French, Washington thus had its man at the helm in Saigon. It was apparently decided, probably jointly by John Foster Dulles and Diem, that Bao Dai had outlived his usefulness and that his removal could be made the occasion for giving the regime a new legal foundation. In any case, while Bao Dai was still nominally head of the government, President Eisenhower pledged United States support to Diem personally. Following this, in October (1954) Diem staged a "national" referendum to ratify his replacement of Bao Dai as "Chief of State." Three days later he proclaimed a "Republic of Vietnam" and appointed himself its first president.

The "free world" has never seen a phonier "revolution"— and it has seen a lot of phony ones. Fewer than 15 percent of those eligible to vote in the referendum did so, and the real power in the country was obviously Ho Chi Minh's government which had only recently crushed the flower of the French army at Dienbienphu. The real situation was finally recognized and publicly stated by Eisenhower in his book *Mandate for Change* dealing with his first four years in the White House:

I am convinced that the French could not win the war because the internal political situation in Vietnam, weak and confused, badly weakened their military position. I have never talked or corresponded with a person knowledgeable in Indochinese affairs who did not agree that had elections been held as of the time of the fighting, possibly 80 percent of the population would have voted for Communist Ho Chi Minh as their leader rather than chief of state Bao Dai. (Quoted by Marquis Child, *The New York Post*, February 16, 1965.)

Obviously a palace coup substituting Diem for Bao Dai could not and did not affect this situation in the slightest. The only difference was that an American puppet took the place of a French puppet. Neither had even the flimsiest claim to be the rightful representative of, or ruler over, the Vietnamese people. That position was firmly held, as it had been after 1945 and has been ever since, by Ho Chi Minh and the government of the Democratic Republic of Vietnam.

So much for the United States claim that it is helping a

"legitimate" government in South Vietnam. The logic is of a piece with that of the boy who shot his mother and father and then asked the judge for mercy on the ground that he was an orphan. To put the matter bluntly, the entire American case for intervention in Vietnam is based on a lie, a Big Lie of truly Hitlerian proportions.

With so much understood, the charge that North Vietnam is violating the Geneva Agreements of 1954 and is guilty of "aggression" can be disposed of very briefly. Anyone who takes the trouble to read the Geneva Agreements cannot fail to understand that their whole purpose was to solve the problem of Vietnam by unifying the country under a popularly elected government. The division of the country at the 17th parallel was envisaged as a purely temporary measure to facilitate the disengagement and demobilization or withdrawal of the fighting forces. It would be terminated by nation-wide elections to be held not later than the summer of 1956. In the meantime, all foreign forces were to be withdrawn and no additional arms were to be sent in from abroad. By flatly refusing even to discuss the prescribed elections, Dulles and Diem not only violated the Agreements; they repudiated the whole conception on which the Agreements were based. It could perhaps be maintained that they at least had the excuse that neither Washington nor Saigon signed the Agreements in the first place and therefore felt no obligation to abide by them. But such a claim, if advanced, would only multiply and compound the impudence and hypocrisy of invoking the Agreements as protection for a separate sovereign state in South Vietnam. The Agreements absolutely did not sanction the division of Vietnam, nor did they provide that North Vietnamese should stay out of South Vietnam. They endorsed the unity of the whole country and provided that foreigners should get out and stay out of the whole country. The only ones who are violating the Geneva Agreements are the Americans, and the only way they can stop violating the Agreements is to get out and let the Vietnamese run their own affairs.

The officially held and propagated American answer to this, of course, is that if the United States should withdraw from Vietnam, the Chinese Communists would take over. This is another Big Lie. The Ho Chi Minh government was in existence some four years before the victory of the Chinese Revolution and had been fighting the French nearly as long by the time the Peking regime established its power down to the Vietnamese border. Ho Chi Minh is no one's puppet, as the French can testify to their sorrow; and there is not one shred of evidence to indicate that the Chinese have ever in any way threatened the independence and sovereignty of the Democratic Republic of Vietnam. The only thing that can bring them into Vietnam is an extension of American attacks on North Vietnam: if this occurs, there is no reason to doubt that the Chinese will enter the war as they did in Korea. But the example of Korea also teaches us that the purpose will be to repel the Americans, not to take over anything. The Chinese long ago withdrew their forces from North Korea; it is only the United States that maintains an army of occupation on Korean soil.

How the War in South Vietnam Started

According to the State Department's White Paper, the present war in South Vietnam—as distinct from the earlier struggle against the French—was started by Ho Chi Minh and his colleagues because they could not tolerate the tremendous economic successes of the Diem regime. This pretty little idyll is so touching that it deserves to be quoted at some length:

Among South Vietnamese, hope rose [after 1954] that their nation could have a peaceful and independent future, free of Communist domination. The country went to work. The years after 1955 were a period of steady progress and growing prosperity. Food production levels of the prewar years were reached and surpassed. While per capita food output was dropping 10 percent in the North from 1956 to 1960, it rose 20 percent in the South. . . .

Production of textiles increased in the South more than 20 percent in one year (1958). In the same year South Vietnam's sugar crop increased more than 100 percent. Despite North Vietnam's vastly larger industrial complex, South Vietnam's per capita gross national product in 1960 was estimated at $110 a person while it was only $70 in the North.

More than 900,000 refugees who had fled from Communist rule in the North were successfully settled in South Vietnam. An agrarian reform program was instituted. The elementary school population nearly quadrupled between 1956 and 1960. And so it went—a record of steady improvement in the lives of the people. It was intolerable for the rulers in Hanoi; under peaceful conditions, the South was outstripping the North. They were losing the battle of peaceful competition and decided to use violence and terror to gain their ends.

The only trouble with this story is that it is a pack of lies, like everything else the United States government puts out about Vietnam. We do not refer to the specific statistics cited. We are in no position to check them, and it makes very little difference how accurate or inaccurate they are. The truth is the whole, as Hegel so correctly remarked, and these are but tiny fragments which could fit into an infinity of wholes.

The real economic history of South Vietnam in the last ten years is, like that of so many other countries in the underdeveloped areas of the "free world," one of missed opportunities, corruption, stagnation, misery, and tragedy. We quote from a letter written to a colleague in the United States by an able liberal American economist who was sent out to Saigon to help the South Vietnamese regime formulate and execute its economic policies. (For obvious reasons the writer must remain anonymous.) The time is late 1960, before the war had reached the pitch of intensity of the last few years and before the political situation in Saigon had begun to fall to pieces—in other words at a time which, in retrospect, can be considered to have been the heyday of Ngo Dinh Diem:

> The economic solution to Vietnam's problems is fairly obvious; it doesn't take a PhD to figure them out. The level of economic analysis does not have to be very sophisticated. The real problem here, which has thus far defied solution, is political and administrative. It is a matter of persuading the appropriate officials to recognize their problems, to face them forthrightly, and to attack them with reasonable energy, dispatch, and competence. For example, one does not have to be very bright to figure out that a net investment rate of 3 to 4 percent of GNP will not provide a rate of growth necessary to keep up with a 3 percent population growth. Nor is it very difficult to conclude that deliberate export of capital [by wealthy Vietnamese] from a capital-poor country is a short-sighted policy. This country has been accumulating 30 to 40 million United States dollars a year of foreign exchange reserves. When I inquire about the motives behind this policy, the reply indicates that the peasant concept of hoarding has been raised to the level of national policy. And so it goes.

I suppose you have read about our recent fireworks. The fact of an attempted coup came as no surprise to us here—although the timing was a surprise. The amount of administrative incompetence and the policies of drift portend eventual collapse of this regime. Unless there is a drastic change in policies and procedures it is just a matter of time. The present government has shown remarkable success in stamping out any democratic opposition but very little competence for stamping out subversive and guerrilla activity. Once again, Uncle Sam has been placed in the position of riding a dead horse.

Poor Uncle Sam! But who placed him in this unenviable position? And why must he go around boasting that his dead horse is winning races? The answers, alas, are as obvious as the accuracy of our economist friend's prediction of things to come. There was no drastic change in policies after 1960; it *was* just a matter of time until the Diem regime collapsed. And, it is now possible to add, collapse was the prelude not to recovery but to sheer political chaos. And all this happened in spite of—or could it by any chance be because of?—the fact that South Vietnam has been, in proportion to its size, one of the biggest recipients of America's economic aid.

As far as the North is concerned, it has certainly had no easy time economically. Cut off from the country's main food-producing regions in the South and unable to tap the bulging storehouses of a rich ally, the people of North Vietnam have been forced to live in austere poverty. At the same time, unlike in the South, it has been poverty combined with justice and hope, and that makes a world of difference. A French journalist, writing in the Paris weekly *L'Express* in 1963, reported after a trip to North Vietnam that

no one is begging for anything and everyone is sharing courageously in the nation's struggle for existence. Not a single functionary is open to bribery. Not a single officer is robbing the state, an occupation so common in all the other countries of Southeast Asia. The sick do not have to pay for hospital care. . . . Poverty in North Vietnam is not the special province of the poor: it is the destiny of all. For this reason it has a dignity that forces the foreigner also to embrace it, sharing what he has. . . . It is a matter of managing without the resources of the South for as long as necessary, of increasing industrial and agricultural production at any cost. (Quoted by Hugh Deane, *The War in Vietnam,* pp. 24-25.)

Not even the most brazen of Washington's paid liars would dare to write of South Vietnam in terms like these. Nor do they care to tell us that North Vietnam's "vastly larger industrial complex," though they have to admit its existence, was mostly built up by heroic efforts in the years that have elapsed since the end of the war against the French—the very same years during which a continuing flood of American goods has ruined much of the industry of the South and thrown tens of thousands of workers out on the streets.

But there is a simple way to test which side is winning "the battle of peaceful competition": remove the barriers separating the two and let the people judge for themselves. That's what the Geneva Agreements aimed to accomplish; it has been consistently advocated by Hanoi; it has been flatly refused by Saigon, and even its advocacy has been made a crime. What more needs to be said?

The State Department's explanation of how the war in South Vietnam started thus turns out to be another Big Lie. But the question itself remains: how *did* it start?

The answer is simple—and grim. The war of liberation against the French also marked the first stages of a genuine social revolution throughout Vietnam, and especially in the countryside, most of which came under the control of the Vietminh during the years of fighting. Many big landholders, both Vietnamese and French, took refuge in the larger towns where they could hide behind French bayonets. The peasants, led and supported by Vietminh cadres who constituted the effective local governments in large parts of the country, proceeded to divide up the larger properties (mostly situated in the South), abolish back rent and taxes, and initiate new forms of cooperation. After the signing of the Geneva Agreements, the regular Vietminh armed forces—some 100,000 strong—withdrew to the North, leaving the French and their puppet troops to maintain order in the South pending the elections prescribed in the Agreements and the subsequent unification of the country. As already noted above, however, the French puppets were soon to become American puppets (perhaps they already were), and neither they nor their new masters had any intention of abiding by the Agreements. As for the French themselves, they simply ran out on their obvious legal and moral obligations under the Agreements, leaving matters entirely in the hands of Messrs. Dulles and Diem.

Under these circumstances the tragedy of South Vietnam followed with iron necessity. Diem set about building a new state machine, drawing largely on bitterly reactionary Catholic refugees from the North and dispossessed landlords in the South—all thirsting for revenge and the recovery of their lost wealth and privileges. A fearful apparatus of counter-revolutionary repression was organized and set in motion. It gradually spread over the countryside, imprisoning, torturing, and killing nationalists and revolutionaries of all descriptions, restoring estates to landlords, installing greedy thugs and bagmen in the seats of local government. Phillipe Devillers, Catholic and anti-Communist, a respected French authority on the history of Vietnam, wrote thus of the years 1957-1959:

A certain sequence of events became almost classical: denunciation, encirclement of villages, searches and raids, arrests of suspects, plundering, interrogations enlivened by torture (even of innocent people), deportation and "regrouping of populations" suspected of intelligence with rebels, etc. (Quoted by Hugh Deane, *The War in Vietnam*, p. 13.)

This is the somber truth which the State Department tries to conceal behind its fancy lies about the "progress and growing prosperity," the "steady improvement in the lives of the people" in the years after 1955. Nor is the picture in any way brightened by the famous land reform cooked up by the Washington "expert" Wolf Ladejinsky and dutifully enacted by Diem and company. As compared to the prewar situation, the Ladejinsky reform represented concessions to the peasantry, even though its main purpose was to promote the growth of a kulak class in the countryside rather than to help the great majority of poor peasants. But as compared to the situation which actually existed in 1954, after the Vietminh had led the peasantry in a real land reform, the Ladejinsky measure was a decisive step backward, an integral part of the counter-revolution.*

---

* On this important point, see Richard Morrock, "Agrarian 'Reform' in South Vietnam," *Monthly Review*, November 1964.

Against this background, is it any wonder that the people of South Vietnam, seeing themselves deprived of the fruits of their victory over the French and feeling on their backs the knout of a new and more ferocious tyranny, should reconstitute their fighting forces and take up again the revolutionary struggle for national independence and economic development? And if the North Vietnamese have helped them, as the White Paper asserts, can anyone who knows the truth about South Vietnam honestly say that they are doing more than fulfilling an unshirkable moral obligation to their brothers and countrymen?

The Crisis of United States Policy

The present crisis of United States policy in Vietnam stems directly from the virtual collapse of the Saigon regime. It is hard to go on pretending that you are helping something that has ceased to exist, and without that pretense there is no plausible reason for the United States to be in South Vietnam. Hence the ineluctable choice: either get out or transform the war into something that maybe can be rationalized and justified.

Before considering these two alternatives, we can quickly dispose of a third which exists only in the minds of certain deluded people—some of whom, to be sure, seem to be high up in the political Establishment. This delusion is that the United States, by attacking and threatening North Vietnam, can somehow create a viable regime in the South and thus permit a return to the status quo ante. There are, as a lawyer might put it, two reasons why this is nonsense: first, the Northerners do not control the revolutionary process in the South and could not halt it even if they wanted to; and second, they obviously would not do it if they could for the simple reason that that would be giving in to blackmail, which would only lay them open to more blackmail. It follows that the state of affairs which exists at the time of writing in early March is by its very nature temporary and transitional. If the United States persists in the policy of air attacks on North Vietnam, the political situation in the South will continue to deteriorate, and the cost in terms of planes and pilots will mount as North Vietnamese air defenses improve as a result of ever greater Chinese and Soviet assistance. This holds regardless of the scale and location of the air attacks: even saturation bombing, as the Korean War proved, can never bring a determined enemy to his knees. Sooner or later the real alternatives will have to be faced: get out or transform the war.

That getting out would be the only rational course to follow is perfectly obvious to anyone who knows the history of the Vietnamese situation and has no axes to grind. And yet, at the time of writing, the probability of this becoming United States policy seems to be small indeed. The reason given, by official and unofficial spokesmen of the Establishment, is that for the United States to withdraw from its "commitment" to Saigon would be an intolerable loss of face and would result in the speedy takeover of all Southeast Asia by the Chinese. This is sheer nonsense on every count. In the first place, the commitment is to its own creature, which is already moribund and will soon be stone dead. In other words, it is by now no more than a commitment by the United States to itself, which can obviously be cancelled at will. Second, getting out of South Vietnam, far from being a loss of face, would greatly enhance the prestige and standing of the United States in the eyes of the vast majority of the world's governments and people. Anyone who thinks this is mere wishful dreaming should ask himself whether France lost face or gained enormously in every way by getting out of Vietnam and Algeria. The answer should be obvious to any schoolboy. And finally, as we have already remarked, the Chinese bogey is just that and nothing more. The Chinese are building socialism, and a socialist society has no interest—and interests always determine policies—in taking over other countries. What they do want, and are perfectly within their rights to want, is friendly, or at any rate non-hostile, neighbors.

It thus appears that the official explanation of why the United States "cannot afford" to get out of Vietnam simply will not stand serious examination. We shall come in a moment to the real reason why it nevertheless refuses to get out. But first we must consider, if only very briefly, the second alternative—transforming the war, which can only mean turning the counter-revolutionary war in South Vietnam into a full-fledged war against North Vietnam and ultimately against China.

There was a time when the United States Army was bitterly opposed to this course, which had been proposed by Dulles and Admiral Radford, head of the Joint Chiefs of Staff, when it became clear that the French were losing the battle of Dienbienphu. The Army objected strongly, for reasons explained by General Matthew B. Ridgway, then Army Chief of Staff, in his memoirs:

In Korea we had learned that air and naval power alone cannot win a war and that inadequate ground forces cannot win one either. It was incredible to me that we had forgotten that bitter lesson so soon—that we were on the verge of making the same tragic error.

That error, thank God, was not repeated. . . . The idea of intervention was abandoned, and it is my belief that the analysis which the Army made and presented to higher authority played a considerable, perhaps a decisive, part in persuading our government not to embark on that tragic adventure. (Quoted in Snow, *The Other Side of the River*, p. 691.)

There is now reason to believe that this opposition on the part of the army has been modified and perhaps abandoned altogether. Most important in this connection is the article by Hanson W. Baldwin in the *New York Times Magazine* of February 21st, advocating a vastly increased commitment of American forces to the war in Vietnam (a position strongly opposed on the editorial page of the *Times* on the same day). Baldwin, the paper's military editor, is known to have close connections in the Pentagon and has not acquired the reputation of being a spokesman for only one of the services. While one cannot be certain, it nevertheless seems likely that Baldwin's advocacy of an all-out effort reflects the views of all three services. Baldwin is under no illusion that a quick or easy victory could be won; on the contrary, what must strike the reader of his article is that apart from a vague notion of stopping "Communist expansionism," he completely fails to define concrete aims, the achievement of which would constitute "victory." After advocating sending more American forces to fight in South Vietnam and greatly stepping up the scope of attacks on North Vietnam, he proceeds as follows:

Meanwhile, it would take years of effort inside South Vietnam itself to reduce the Vietcong to manageable proportions.

Much larger, and better led, South Vietnamese forces would be necessary. They would have to be supplemented by United States ground troops—perhaps in small numbers at first, but more later, particularly if North Vietnamese regular forces and Chinese soldiers joined the Vietcong.

How many United States soldiers would be needed is uncertain—probably a minimum of three to six divisions (utilized chiefly in battalion or brigade-size units), possibly as many as 10 or 12 divisions. Including Air Force, Navy and suppporting units perhaps 200,000 to 1,000,000 Americans would be fighting in Vietnam.

Obviously, this would mean a Korean-type conflict, a major war, no matter what euphemisms would be used. Nor could we wage it in the present "business-as-usual" economy. We would require partial mobilization, vastly beefed-up military production. Many weaknesses in our military structure would need strengthening. Even so, we could not anticipate quick success. The war would be long, nasty and wearing.

One may well wonder whether Mr. Baldwin is not too optimistic. What makes him think that much larger and better led South Vietnamese forces can be pressed into the service of an American enterprise of this kind? Is it not more likely that the disintegration of the South Vietnamese regime, and with it its armies, will simply be accelerated? And does he imagine that the North Vietnamese and Chinese, once involved, are going to quit while American soldiers are still on the mainland of Asia? Is he not really offering us a formula for either endless war or American defeat?

In an impressive hour-long television interview near the end of February, Walter Lippmann, one of the few rational voices coming from the American ruling class these days, predicted that if the war party has its way and the United States gets involved in a big war on the Asian mainland, the "war hawks" will be happy but "the people will weep." Prophetic words, we fear, for where is the evidence that Lyndon B. Johnson, so lately the shining knight of the liberals and their leftist camp-followers, has either the principles or the courage to stand up to the war-bent military-industrial establishment?

What is it that impels this apparently unstoppable drive to Armageddon—and beyond it to disaster? Can it be that South Vietnam, or even all of Southeast Asia, is such a vital interest of the American ruling class? No, hardly.* There is a much larger question involved in the struggle in Vietnam: can a country fight its way out of the "free world"—that is, the free-enterprise world, the world open to exploitation by American capitalism—in direct confrontation with the most powerful imperialist nation? China and Cuba fought their way out, but only against the local lieutenants of the supreme imperial power. In Vietnam it is different. There the imperial power has assumed direct responsibility for keeping one half of a relatively small and very backward country from breaking out of the free world—and it is failing. It is this, and not simply the "loss" of South Vietnam, which the rulers of the United States find intolerable. If South Vietnam can do it, why not Brazil or Nigeria or Turkey or Iran? Would it not be the beginning of the end of the free world, that indispensable *Lebensraum* of American capitalism?

Cyrus Sulzberger, the foreign affairs columnist of the *New York Times,* put his finger on the nub of the problem when he wrote (March 3):

> The heart of the crisis is not truly in Vietnam. The quintessential problem is how to defeat revolutionary warfare. Elsewhere in Asia and Africa [why leave out Latin America?] we will continue to face the threat of this technique no matter what happens to the Vietnamese. That is inescapable.
> Not merely the aggressive Chinese but the relatively less aggressive Russians are committed to sponsor "wars of liberation." Despite this glaring truth, both in weapons and in training, we are basically prepared alone for the war our adversaries don't intend to start.

The implication that there are some different kinds of weapons and training which would enable the United States to defeat revolutionary warfare is of course merely one of those myths which the American ruling class likes to interpose between itself and reality. The truth is that it cannot be done. All the myths are wearing thin, and the time is approaching

---

*We are of course aware that many of the "war hawks" believe that a war against China is sooner or later inevitable and that the sooner it comes the better. This has been true ever since 1949, however, and we know of no evidence that they are more powerful now than they were when MacArthur was their leader during the Korean War.

when the would-be gods of Washington will find reality staring them in the face. In Vietnam they sense it even if they do not yet understand it. Hence the seeming paradox which is really no paradox at all that the richest and most heavily armed nation in world history is striking out like a desperate cornered rat.

They can yet kill many thousands, perhaps millions of innocent people. But Americans will be killed too, and in increasing numbers. If it takes, according to Hanson Baldwin, from two hundred thousand to a million men to fight in little Vietnam, how many will it take when the rest of Asia, Africa, and Latin America join the insurrection against imperialist rule, as sooner or later they must?

We leave it to the Hanson Baldwins to make their own grisly calculations. In the meantime, one thing is as certain as anything can be in this uncertain world: the road on which our leaders are now travelling in Vietnam leads not only, as Walter Lippmann so rightly says, to bitter tears. Its destination is national exhaustion and ruin. The course of the Decline and Fall of the American Empire has now been charted for all to see.

A New Phase Opens

The last few weeks have witnessed developments directly and indirectly related to the war in Vietnam which may well turn out to be of historic significance. Perhaps it is superfluous to say that we are not referring to Washington's "peace offensive" or the resumption of United States bombing of North Vietnam. The "peace offensive" was as phony as a $9-bill from the outset, and the bombing pause was merely a part of it. These events have changed nothing, and on a world scale it is quite possible, maybe even probable, that they have done more to expose than to obscure the true nature of United States involvement in Vietnam.

The Illusion of Omnipotence

The developments to which we do refer add up to what looks like the beginning of a reappraisal on the part of the United States ruling class of its real position in the world.

It has of course long been obvious to anyone with a sense of history that the United States is very far from being omnipotent. To mention only events of the last two decades: The revolution triumphed in China despite massive American military and economic support for Chiang Kai-shek and his numerically vastly superior armies. The attempt to conquer North Korea was decisively repulsed. Cuba escaped from the American imperial prison right under the nose of the warder. These were all humiliating defeats for the United States ruling class and should have been more than enough to set it to thinking seriously about the limits of its power. But apart from a few Cassandras like Walter Lippmann and mavericks like Wayne Morse who were never seriously listened to, the lessons of these defeats of the recent past were either ignored or rationalized out of existence by the ruling class and its ideologues. China was "lost" because of a Communist plot in the State Department or because American soldiers were not committed to Chiang's cause; the Korean setback could have been averted if MacArthur had been allowed to bomb China; the Cuban Revolution succeeded only because Washington was too slow in understanding its nature and hence did not take preventive measures in good time. Reasoning in ways like this led not to pondering the *limits* of American power but rather to the conclusion that the solution lay in dropping all restraints on the *uses* of American power. Commit whatever American forces may be needed to win; permit no "privileged sanctuaries"; prevent revolutionary takeovers by direct military intervention—*these* are the lessons the American ruling class drew from the failures of the postwar period.

It must be recognized that certain events, considered (in typical American fashion) outside of their proper geographical and temporal context, have seemed to confirm the correctness of this diagnosis. Thus the effort of the Congo to win genuine independence was squelched, and a full-scale invasion of the Dominican Republic prevented the armed people of Santo Domingo from settling accounts once and for all with as cruel and corrupt a military machine as Latin America has ever known. But in Vietnam it has been different. The counter-revolutionary puppet regime inherited from the French in 1954 fared no better under its new masters than it had under the old. When despite lavish American military "advice" and financial aid, the Saigon government collapsed as Chiang Kai-shek's had done a decade and a half earlier, the Americans applied their new-found wisdom by sending in massive sea, air, and ground forces to take over the bulk of the fighting. And North Vietnam, having been proclaimed the instigator and supplier of the war in the South, was subjected to increasingly heavy bombardment. Here at last the supposedly foolproof formula for victory—commit American power directly and define unilaterally the terms on which it will be used—was put to the test. One year later, the results are known to all. In the words of the Mansfield Report:

Insofar as the military situation is concerned, the large-scale introduction of U.S. forces and their entry into combat has blunted but not turned back the drive of the Vietcong. The latter have

responded to the increased American role with a further strengthening of their forces by local recruitment in the south and reinforcements from the north and a general stepping up of military
activity. As a result the lines remain drawn in South Vietnam
in substantially the same pattern as they were at the outset of the
increased U.S. commitment. What has changed basically is the
scope and intensity of the struggle and the part which is being
played by the forces of the United States and those of North
Vietnam.*

It must not be assumed of course that the full meaning of
the failure in Vietnam has been grasped by the American
oligarchy. What is doubtless a large majority of its members,
including leading figures in the Johnson administration, still
cling to the old illusion of American omnipotence. If a quarter
of a million troops (approximately the present number counting
Naval personnel) are not enough to ensure victory, throw in a
half a million or a million—whatever may be necessary. And
if bombing North Vietnam produces no results, extend the
attacks to Laos and Cambodia and as a last resort to China
itself. This is apparently the strategic doctrine which continues
to govern American conduct of the war in Vietnam; and it
would be unrealistic to expect it to be seriously modified in the
near future. Nevertheless, a change *has* taken place during the
last year, and one of great potential importance for the longer
run. It is no longer only Cassandras and mavericks who view
the present course of United States policy with alarm: skeptic-
ism, doubt, and even downright disillusion have invaded the
inner circles of the ruling establishment. This can be seen most
clearly in two documents published since the first of the year—
the Mansfield Report cited above, and the Gavin letter.

In evaluating the first of these documents it must be kept
in mind that Mansfield himself is the Senate majority leader,
very much a part of the Johnson team and personally close
to the President. The Report carefully refrains from any overt

---

* *The Vietnam Conflict: The Substance and the Shadow*, Report of
Senator Mike Mansfield, Senator Edmund S. Muskie, Senator Daniel K.
Inouye, Senator George D. Aiken, Senator J. Caleb Boggs to the Foreign
Relations Committee, United States Senate, January 6, 1966, p. 11. A copy
of this important document can be obtained by writing to Senator Mans-
field or to one of your own Senators.

criticism of administration policies and actions and throughout employs the language of muted understatement. These facts only make the more devastating its conclusions, from which it seems worthwhile to quote at considerable length:

Despite the great increase in American military commitment, it is doubtful in view of the acceleration of Vietcong efforts that the constricted position now held in Vietnam by the Saigon government can continue to be held for the indefinite future, let alone extended, without a further augmentation of American forces on the ground. Indeed if present trends continue, there is no assurance as to what ultimate increase in American military commitment will be required before the conflict is terminated. For the fact is that under present terms of reference and as the war has evolved, the question is not one of applying increased U.S. pressure to a defined military situation but rather of pressing against a military situation which is, in effect, open ended. How open is dependent on the extent to which North Vietnam and its supporters are willing and able to meet increased force by increased force. All of mainland Southeast Asia, at least, cannot be ruled out as a potential battlefield. . . .

Even if the war remains substantially within its present limits, there is little foundation for the expectation that the government of Vietnam in Saigon will be able, in the near future, to carry a much greater burden than it is now carrying. This is in no sense a reflection on the caliber of the current leaders of Vietnam. But the fact is that they are, as other Vietnamese governments have been over the past decade, at the beginning of a beginning in dealing with the problems of popular mobilization in support of the government. They are starting, moreover, from a point considerably behind that which prevailed at the time of President Diem's assassination. Under present concepts and plans, then, what lies ahead is literally a vast and continuing undertaking in social engineering in the wake of such military progress as may be registered. And for many years to come this task will be very heavily dependent on U.S. foreign aid.

The basic concept of present American policy with respect to Vietnam casts the United States in the role of support of the Vietnamese government and people. This concept becomes more difficult to maintain as the military participation of the United States undergoes rapid increase. Yet a change in the basic concept could have a most unfortunate impact upon the Vietnamese people and the world at large. What is involved here is the necessity for the greatest restraint in word and action, lest the concept be eroded and the war drained of a purpose with meaning to the people of Vietnam.

This danger is great, not only because of the military realities of the situation but also because, with few exceptions, assistance has not been and is not likely to be forthcoming for the war effort in South Vietnam from nations other than the United States. On the contrary, as it now appears, the longer the war continues in its present pattern and the more it expands in scope, the greater will become the strain upon the relations of the United States with allies both in the Far East and in Europe.

Many nations are deeply desirous of an end to this conflict as quickly as possible. Few are specific as to the manner in which this end can be brought about or the shape it is likely to take. In any event, even though other nations in certain circumstances may be willing to play a third-party role in bringing about negotiations, any prospects for effective negotiations at this time (and they are slim) are likely to be largely dependent on the initiatives and efforts of the combatants.

Negotiations at this time, moreover, if they do come about, and if they are accompanied by a cease-fire and standfast, would serve to stabilize a situation in which a majority of the population remains under nominal government control but in which dominance of the countryside rests largely in the hands of the Vietcong. What might eventually materialize through negotiations from this situation cannot be foreseen at this time with any degree of certainty.

This is not, to say the least, a very satisfactory prospect. What needs also to be borne in mind, however, is that the visible alternative at this time and under present terms of reference is the indefinite expansion and intensification of the war which will require the continuous introduction of additional U.S. forces. The end of that course cannot be foreseen, either, and there are no grounds for optimism that the end is likely to be reached within the confines of South Vietnam or within the very near future.

In short, such choices as may be open are not simple choices. They are difficult and painful choices and they are beset with many imponderables. The situation, as it now appears, offers only the very slim prospect of a just settlement by negotiations or the alternative prospect of a continuance of the conflict in the direction of a general war on the Asian mainland.

Stripped of provisos and qualifications, all of which are stated so tentatively and weakly as to give the impression of being mere window dressing, this pretty plainly says:

(1) The Saigon regime has virtually ceased to function. Nevertheless, we must pretend otherwise in order to try to make the Vietnamese believe that there is some meaningful purpose in continuing the war.

(2) Any serious negotiations would have to be with the National Liberation Front since of course it is the main "combatant" on the other side.

(3) Internationally, the war is isolating the United States from its allies all over the world.

(4) The way things are going now, the United States is headed for a bigger and bigger land war, spreading first to all of Southeast Asia and eventually becoming a "general war on the Asian mainland"—in other words a war with China.

(5) The only thing that can avert these dire consequences is a change in basic policy (euphemistically called "terms of reference").

The Report does not state, or even hint at, the logical conclusion from its conclusions—that the only way to get out of the mess in Vietnam is to recognize the NLF and negotiate a withdrawal, saving as much face as possible. But by making that conclusion obvious to any literate person with normal powers of reasoning, it nevertheless performs a most useful function. It shows that the illusion of omnipotence which has so long protected United States global policy from rational criticism is beginning to crumble in the very highest political circles.

Like the Mansfield Report, the Gavin letter* must be evaluated in the light of its author's background and position. A paratroop commander during the Second World War, Gavin subsequently rose to the top echelon of the Pentagon hierarchy as Chief of Plans and Operations in the Department of the Army. A champion of new technological concepts of warfare, Gavin quarreled with what he considered to be the conservative military policies of the Eisenhower administration and retired in 1958. After a period as Ambassador to France under Kennedy, he became Chairman of the Board and chief executive officer of Arthur D. Little, Inc., which is probably the largest and best known firm specializing in research and development work for private business and government. Gavin has thus not only had a distinguished military career but has also had diplo-

---

* "A Communication on Vietnam" from General James M. Gavin, *Harper's Magazine,* February 1966, pp. 16-21.

matic experience and in his present position is a full-fledged member of what C. Wright Mills called the corporate elite. It is unlikely that the views he expresses are only his own.

Stating at the outset that he is writing "solely from a military-technical point of view," Gavin makes two points which complement and illuminate the findings of the Mansfield Report. In his own words:

Today we have sufficient force in South Vietnam to hold several enclaves on the coast, where sea and air power can be made fully effective. . . . However, we are stretching these resources beyond reason in our endeavors to secure the entire country of South Vietnam from the Vietcong penetration. . . . If our objective is to secure all of South Vietnam, then forces should be deployed on the 17th parallel and along the Cambodian border adequate to do this. In view of the nature of the terrain, it might be necessary to extend our defenses on the 17th parallel to the Mekong River, and across part of Thailand. Such a course would take many times as much force as we now have in Vietnam.

To increase the bombing and to bomb Hanoi—or even Peking—will add to our problems rather than detract from them, and it will not stop the penetrations of North Vietnam troops into the South. Also, if we were to quadruple, for example, our combat forces there, we would then anticipate the intervention of Chinese "volunteers" and the reopening of the Korean front. This seems to be the ultimate prospect of the course that we are now on.

Thus, just to conquer South Vietnam, which of course is now largely in the hands of the NLF, would require "many times" the quarter of a million troops already there; and expanded bombing outside South Vietnam would create more problems than it would solve. What Gavin does not tell us is the magnitude of the American commitment which would be required when, as both he and the Mansfield Report predict, the attempt to secure South Vietnam leads to full-scale war with China. But common sense tells us that if securing South Vietnam implies an increase of many times the present force, war with China will raise that by another factor of many times. Clearly, what is now in prospect—i.e., highly probable if the present course is persisted in—is a mobilization and commitment of manpower to the Asian mainland comparable in magnitude to the *total* effort of the Second World War. It follows quite logically, in the words of the French Gaullist paper

Paris Jour, that "One of the consequences of the pursuit of the conflict in Southeast Asia which is no longer doubted in the chancelleries . . . will be a veritable 'disengagement' of American forces—but not of the United States herself—on every other front covering nearly every other continent." (Quoted in the *New York Times*, February 6, 1966.) Thus, by an ironic twist, the illusion of omnipotence threatens to turn into the reality of world-wide impotence! Is it any wonder that the illusion itself is beginning to wear thin?

There are of course other indications that this is indeed occurring, and one in particular deserves notice before we leave this subject. Shortly after the publication of the Mansfield Report on January 6, there took place an abrupt change in the attitude and policy statements of high Republican Party figures toward the war in Vietnam. As late as January 7, Senate Minority Leader Everett Dirksen, speaking at a news conference, voiced the familiar Republican "tough" line on Vietnam. "There is no substitute for victory," he said, and the United States and South Vietnamese forces should force the Vietcong "to lay down their arms." He stopped short of openly advocating the bombing of Hanoi, but said that Haiphong was another matter since it was the main seaport through which the North Vietnamese received their supplies. Less than a week later, on January 11, he was singing a different tune. Here are excerpts from a Washington dispatch by E. W. Kenworthy which appeared in the *New York Times* of January 12 (omissions not indicated):

Everett McKinley Dirksen, the Senate Republican leader, warned party colleagues today to consider the possible consequences before advocating the bombing of Hanoi and its harbor city Haiphong.

The Illinoisan delivered his warning indirectly, but effectively, by reading to the Senate Republican Conference a sentence from the report on Vietnam made last weekend by the Democratic leader, Mike Mansfield of Montana, and four other Senators who visited Vietnam with him. This sentence read:

"It is considered by some that Saigon with its many vulnerabilities to sabotage and terrorism and Hanoi with its exposure to air attack are mutual hostages, one for the other."

In a news conference later, Mr. Dirksen said he had simply read the sentence without expanding on it. But for reporters he drew a vivid picture of United States and allied freighters sitting at anchor in the Saigon River and the Vietcong positioned with heavy mortars on the other side of the river.

"Suppose you drop a flock of eggs on Hanoi," he went on. "They can destroy Saigon. There is the equation."

Mr. Dirksen did not withdraw what he said last Friday [January 7] about "capitulation before peace." But he did not press this argument today. Instead, the burden of his remarks was that escalation might turn the war into an American war and that advocates of escalation should consider the cost in blood.

Pressed on what had brought about the seeming change in his attitude, he referred to the Mansfield report, saying it carried the names of five Senators, two of them Republicans, George D. Aiken of Vermont and J. Caleb Boggs of Delaware.

There is no reason to doubt the importance of the Mansfield Report in causing this remarkable about-face, but it would certainly be naive to assume that there was nothing more involved than Dirksen's reading the report and changing his mind. One must assume that high-level policy conferences took place, participated in by leading Republicans both in and out of Congress, that certain basic political decisions were reached, and that Dirksen's new position reflected these decisions. More light on the nature of these decisions was thrown in subsequent press reports from Washington, of which the most revealing that has come to our attention is one by Tom Wicker in the *New York Times* of February 2 (omissions not indicated):

Republican Congressional strategists believe divisions within the Democratic party and the prospect of an expanding land war in Vietnam may be giving them a winning political issue against President Johnson.

They believe the country may eventually turn against a President whose party does not fully support him and whose war policy may produce long casualty lists without military victory or a negotiated settlement.

To take political advantage of this, the Republican leaders are pulling back from direct criticism of the Johnson policy and are de-emphasizing their former "hard line" on how the war should be conducted.

Since Mr. Johnson is Commander-in-Chief, they reason, they will not insist that he follow a particular course or attempt to impose a Republican strategy on him. The net effect, these leaders hope, will be to concentrate political as well as constitutional responsibility for the war squarely on the President.

By 1968, they believe, Mr. Johnson may be in political trouble as a result of bearing that responsibility and the country may be ready to turn to a Republican, just as it turned to General of the Army Dwight D. Eisenhower in 1952 during the Korean War.

In that event, some Republican strategists do not rule out the possibility that their party might run a presidential candidate who would promise to end the war by negotiations, as did General Eisenhower. They do not want to foreclose any possibility by insisting on a Republican alternative policy, on which they would have to campaign in the future.

This new approach to the politics of the Vietnamese war is in clear contrast to the earlier Republican approach of urging a stronger military policy and warning against a negotiated settlement.

It reflects the general political uncertainty about the depth of public support for the Vietnamese war, as well as a desire to maintain a flexible position of support for the Commander-in-Chief without being pinned to a fixed policy for winning the war.

It also reflects some Republicans' resentment at the President, who they believe has sought their support for "tough" measures like bombing the North but who has not attempted to associate them with more immediately popular developments like the pause in the bombing and the "peace offensive."

This is a shrewd political strategy—provided the basic assumption on which it rests is sound. This assumption evidently is that the United States cannot win the war in Vietnam at any price in terms of casualties and sacrifices which the American people are willing to pay. That the very Republican leaders, men like Dirksen and House Minority Leader Gerald Ford who until a month ago were the chief advocates of escalation, are now prepared to make this assumption the foundation of their political strategy is surely evidence of a remarkable degree of awakening in the American ruling class to the realities of the world situation. The illusion of omnipotence is not yet dead, but there seems little doubt that the war in Vietnam has dealt it a blow from which it can never recover.

The Twilight of Lyndon B. Johnson

If all this is so, one conclusion emerges with crystal clarity: the number one casualty of the Vietnamese war is going to be Lyndon B. Johnson. Whether or not he and his co-architects of United States policy in the Far East (chief among them McNamara, Rusk, and Bundy) understand the implications of what they are doing makes little difference. This is a classic case of "they're damned if they do and damned if they don't." They can't pull out of Vietnam without in effect admitting that they have been wrong—profoundly, horribly, disastrously wrong. And they can't continue on their present course without plunging the country ever deeper into a ruinous Asian war. In either case their political leadership will sooner or later be proved a failure on a scale for which the history of the United States provides no precedent. They will leave the political stage in well deserved disgrace.

Maybe Johnson senses this, for his actions of the last two months would be difficult to explain except as a manifestation of political panic. He has been steadily escalating the war in accordance with the dictates of the Pentagon planners: according to James Reston, "present plans . . . call for doubling the American manpower commitment in the present calendar year, from 200,000 to 400,000, and going up to 600,000 in 1967." (*New York Times*, February 9.) But Johnson does this not only with a bad conscience but seemingly without any conviction that it will solve anything. So for the bad conscience he puts on a phony peace offensive, and to win the war he prescribes (as Eisenhower and Kennedy had already done on innumerable occasions) a dose of social reform in South Vietnam, apparently not noticing that he thereby concedes that the war is really a revolution against the system and not "aggression" from the North.* The resulting policy amalgam is almost unbelievably weird. To quote again from Reston's February 9 column:

Everything in the Johnson strategy seems to be done in twos—something for the hawks and something for the doves; bomb

---

* This admission is the only real political content of the genuinely comical "Declaration of Honolulu" subscribed to by the Washington and Saigon governments. This subversive document is so full of incitation to "social revolution" (the expression occurs no fewer than four times in less than two columns of newsprint) that its authors, were they less exalted personages, would run the risk of being arrested under the Smith Act in the United States and of being summarily executed in South Vietnam.

North Vietnam and go to the UN Security Council; step up the military forces and increase the pacification program and send Hubert Humphrey to Saigon at the same time; criticize the Saigon government in private and commit American power and prestige to it in public; assert that America cannot police the world but proclaim simultaneously that tyranny in the jungles of continental Asia is just as much America's concern as tyranny and subjugation of the peoples of Europe.

These are the actions of a desperate man who realizes that he has lost control of the situation and is, in Reston's expression, "thrashing about" in a frantic search for some way to recoup. Unfortunately for Lyndon B. Johnson, his chances of finding one are very poor and getting poorer with every hike of the escalator: the higher up the harder it is to get off, and at the top there is nothing but a bottomless abyss.

Is There a Way Out for the American Ruling Class?

That Johnson's political life and reputation are at stake in the Vietnamese war does not mean, of course, that it is impossible for the American ruling class to escape from the trap it is now caught in. As Lenin once said, there is no such thing as a situation from which there is no way out. And the fact that the escape, if there is to be one, will take place under a different political leadership is not only not surprising; it is standard operating procedure for a bourgeois democracy.*

It may even be that the timing of events will turn out to be favorable to the search for an escape. It has taken several years of escalating the war with only negative results to convince a substantial part of the ruling class that the United States cannot "win" in Vietnam. It may be that another two years will be enough to generalize this conviction and to set the stage for a change in leadership and policy. As we have already seen, the

---

* Illustrations from recent history abound: Roosevelt had to unseat Hoover before any serious measures could be taken to overcome the crisis brought on by the Great Depression; Churchill replaced Chamberlain when the Nazis broke through the Maginot Line; it was Eisenhower, not Truman, who ended the Korean War; Mendès-France had to be brought in to liquidate the French war in Vietnam after the defeat at Dienbienphu; Anthony Eden gave way to Harold Macmillan when the Suez adventure collapsed; and it was only de Gaulle's return to power that opened the way to a settlement of the Algerian War.

Republicans are beginning to think in terms of such an eventuality, and the course now being followed by Johnson and company seems certain to enhance the attractiveness of the political strategy which it implies. The 1968 election may come just in time to enable the shift to be made by normal political processes.

As to the terms of a settlement which can bring the war to an end, there can be no doubt whatever: the United States will have to get out of Vietnam and leave the country to its own people. The Vietnamese, having been twice cheated of a victory won by their own blood and tears—by the French in 1945-1946 and again by the Americans after 1954—will certainly not lay down their arms again unless and until they have iron-clad guarantees that this time their independence will be total and genuine. All talk of any other end to the war is either tactical disguise or based on a continuing failure to understand the real situation. This is especially true of what has come to be known as the "enclaves" policy advocated by Gavin, George Kennan, Walter Lippmann, and other critics of the Johnson administration. If the passive holding of enclaves is looked upon as a face-saving device and a halfway house on the way to withdrawal, as the wiser of these critics undoubtedly intend, then the policy makes perfectly good sense. But if it is hoped in this way to get the Vietnamese to accept an American presence, no matter what its shape or form, then the enclaves policy is a delusion on a par with all the other delusions about Vietnam which reality has been so pitilessly destroying.

The next two years will obviously be decisive. For the first time the American ruling class is beginning to wake up to the real costs and consequences of an endlessly expanding war in Asia. It has two years to make up its collective mind whether it wants to cut its losses. If it decides that it does, it has available the political means to effect a change in policy: an attractive Republican candiate can be run in 1968 on a platform promising to end the war. His election, after two more years of mounting draft calls and casualties, can be taken as a virtual certainty.

The alternative is a drift into total war, total regimentation at home—and, sooner or later, total disaster.

Why Vietnam?

In Chapter 5 of *The Age of Imperialism*, Harry Magdoff established beyond any possibility of doubt that the United States economy is not only heavily involved in a variety of activities beyond the country's borders; it is crucially and decisively dependent on its foreign involvements. Further, it is self-evident that the profitability of these involvements is positively and strongly correlated with the degree of control exercised by the corporations and individuals concerned over the markets and fields of investment in which they operate. If, finally, we take account of that iron law of capitalism, that every profit-making enterprise is under permanent pressure to expand,* we reach the conclusion that United States capitalism is and must be continuously seeking not only to maintain but to extend the scope of its foreign involvements and to strengthen its control over the economies and societies into which it penetrates. It is this relentless drive to expand and dominate which is commonly, and quite correctly, considered to be the essence of imperialsm. One can say without fear of exaggeration that if this is not understood there is no possibility of understanding what is happening in the world today.

A necessary condition for understanding what is happening in the world, however, is not a sufficient condition for understanding specific events and situations. The fact that the United States is fighting a major war in Vietnam, for example,

---

* An admirable statement of this law comes from the latest annual report of the Rockwell-Standard Corporation, a major manufacturer of machinery, aircraft, and automotive parts: "The only real security for this company or any other company is through healthly, continuous and vigorous growth. A company is just like a human being. When it stops growing, when it can't replenish itself through growth, then it starts to deteriorate. . . . There is no security where there is no opportunity for growth and development and continual improvement." *Rockwell-Standard Corporation 1965 Annual Report*, Rockwell-Standard Corporation, 300 Sixth Avenue, Pittsburgh, Pennsylvania.

cannot be explained as a simple consequence or outgrowth of economic pressure to expand. To be sure, American economic interests in Vietnam exist and are growing more important, but on a world scale they are relatively small and likely to remain so. It would make no sense to assert that the United States is waging a war which is already costing upward of $20 billion, is tying down a substantial and growing proportion of the country's trained military manpower, and might escalate into a global catastrophe, merely to protect a few hundred million dollars worth of trade and investment in Vietnam.

The problem must be posed in different terms. As already noted, the essence of imperialism—that without which it would be something totally different—is the drive to economic expansion and domination. But imperialism is much more than that. It is an entire social order—a set of class relations, a mode of government, an ideological superstructure—and, what is more, a social order which is riddled with conflicts and contradictions. But even if all this is taken into account, the concrete behavior of imperialism still cannot be understood. For imperialism is not alone in the world, nor does its environment consist only of weaker societies which it can prey upon at will, as was once the case. During the last half century a rival and antagonistic social order, capable of absorbing and utilizing and developing modern science and technology, has arisen to challenge the supremacy, and indeed the very existence, of imperialism. These two world orders exist in perpetual competition and conflict, and the pressures generated by their continuous interaction play an important and often a decisive role in shaping the internal processes of both.

Against this background, an event like the war in Vietnam can be seen to be an extremely complicated phenomenon which has no easily defined cause or set of causes. It is rather the result of the subtle fusing of a large number of forces and tendencies. And it has a history, which means that even a fully adequate explanation of how it began—if such is conceivable— might be only a part of an explanation of its present scope and possible future development. Under these circumstances the answer to the question "Why Vietnam?" which Americans are asking with increasing frequency and urgency cannot be either simple or complete. Nevertheless an attempt to provide an answer must be made.*

The first thing to remember about the war in Vietnam is that it began as a war by the French to reconquer their Indo-Chinese colonies. That was in 1946, three years before the victory of the Chinese Revolution. It was only after the latter event that the Americans became seriously involved, first in support of the French and their puppet Bao Dai and later, after the defeat of the French at Dienbienphu, on their own and with their own puppet, Ngo Dinh Diem.

From the outset American intervention served a dual purpose, to check the spread of the Asian revolution and to gather into the American neocolonial fold a potentially very rich area which the older European empires could no longer hold onto. It is of the utmost importance to understand that in both respects much more than Vietnam was (and is) at stake. The revolution, enormously strengthened by its epochal triumph in China, was obviously on the order of the day, or at latest the morrow, not only in Vietnam itself but also in the whole of mainland Southeast Asia and the vast island clusters of Indonesia and the Philippines. A look at the map of the region is enough to show the central strategic position of the Vietnamese "hump" which juts out into the South China Sea from roughly Hué in the north to Saigon in the south. Any one wanting to build up a strong counter-revolutionary base and pole of attraction in that part of the world would naturally select South Vietnam as the locus of the effort. And the historical background of faltering French colonialism provided the Americans with the needed opening, first for their financial and political influence and later for their military take-over. As for the enlargement of the American neocolonial empire, that would almost automatically follow success in Vietnam. For it has long

---

* Martin Nicolaus undoubtedly reflects a widespread feeling on the American Left when he writes that "at nearly every meeting where the war is debated, there is some intelligent and sincere person who pops the embarrasing question: 'Well, if we're not in Vietnam to defend the people's freedom, tell me—why *are* we there?' It would be a big step forward if one knew how to reply with something more than a few mumbled phrases about 'bad advice,' a shrug of the shoulders, and an honest concession of ignorance." *Viet-Report*, June/July 1966, p. 28.

been evident that the days of the older imperialisms in South
east Asia are numbered and that the only alternatives befor
the region are revolution or increasing dependency on American
economic and military power. If the revolution could be check
ed, the imperial fruits would ripen and fall of their own accord

When the Americans openly intervened in Vietnam, afte
the Geneva Conference in 1954, they undoubtedly expected a
relatively easy victory. By refusing to sign the Geneva agree
ments, they laid the groundwork for an "independent" South
Vietnam which was supposed to be the center from which
American influence and power would radiate through the whole
region. For a few years everything seemed to proceed accord
ing to plan. Diem was installed in power in Saigon and began
the bloody work of undoing the revolution which had taken
place in the countryside during the long war against the French
All that was needed to consolidate a huge American empir
in Southeast Asia, it seemed, was plenty of money and patience

What upset this pretty scheme, of course, was the resistanc
of the South Vietnamese people. When they realized that the
Geneva agreements were being ignored by Diem and his Ameri
can masters and that they were being robbed of the hard-won
gains of the 1946-1954 period, they reformed their fighting
ranks and resumed the struggle where it had been broken off
after the victory at Dienbienphu. This was the beginning of
the war in Vietnam as we know it today.

By the time the war erupted again in Vietnam, the Ameri
cans had already acquired a good deal of experience in coping
with conflicts of this kind, and they naturally believed that
they could liquidate the Vietnamese guerrillas as they had the
Greek partisans and the Philippine Huks—through arming and
training and "advising" a native counter-revolutionary army
Once again however, they reckoned without the Vietnamese
people who now showed themselves to be among history'
greatest masters of the art of revolutionary guerrilla warfare
Most of the countryside was wrested from Diem's armies, and
Diem himself was overthrown, his usefulness to the American
exhausted. There followed a period of rapid political and mili
tary deterioration for the Saigon regime, with one puppe
quickly following another into oblivion. As 1964 drew to a

close, the end was clearly in sight: within a few months at most, all South Vietnam would be in the hands of the National Liberation Front.

Up to this point there is surely no mystery about the answer to "Why Vietnam?" The United States was doing what it had been trying to do elsewhere, sometimes successfully (e.g. Greece) and sometimes not (e.g. China), ever since the declaration of the Truman Doctrine in 1947: check the spread of revolution and, at the same time and not so incidentally, prepare the way for incorporating new regions into the American empire. Up to the end of 1964 the main American investment in the effort was money, with most of the fighting being done by native conscripts and mercenaries.

The collapse of the Saigon regime and the imminent takeover of South Vietnam by the NLF created a new situation and forced Washington to make a choice: either withdraw the American military "advisers" and write off South Vietnam, or pour in additional forces and Americanize the war. As everyone knows, the decision was made in favor of the latter alternative.

In the nature of the case, however, this was not and could not have been a simple decision to replace South Vietnamese administrators and soldiers with Americans, leaving everything else unchanged.*

---

* Lest we be accused of relying on hindsight in making this statement, we quote from an editorial we wrote a full year before the turning point came: "As long as the war is being conducted by a South Vietnamese government, its objective, however unattainable, is unambiguously defined: to liquidate the guerrillas and restore law and order. . . . But if the local government collapses [as we had already predicted it soon would], what will the role of the United States then be? Can it continue to pursue the same war aims? The answer is that the United States would then assume the posture of a military occupier, and the purpose of continuing the war as a strictly South Vietnamese affair could only be the maintenance of an out-and-out military colony on the Asian mainland. Let us be perfectly clear about one thing: in the world of today this would not be a tenable position for the United States to be in. . . . In order to justify continuation of the war, new and broader aims would have to be espoused and the character of the war would have to be correspondingly changed." (See above, pp. 37-42.)

The United States could not fight a civil war in another country, nor could it retreat to the nineteenth century and frankly avow an ambition to establish an old-fashioned colony on the Asian mainland. The only alternative was to charge aggression by North Vietnam and extend the war north of the 17th parallel. These steps were accordingly taken in February 1965, with the issuance of the famous White Paper (entitled "Aggression from the North: The Record of North Vietnam's Campaign to Conquer South Vietnam") and the almost simultaneous beginning of regular bombing raids on North Vietnam. From that time on the Americanization of the war proceeded with great rapidity until now, less than two years later, the number of United States military personnel in and around Vietnam is approaching the half million mark and the American casualty rate is running as high as twice that of the South Vietnamese forces.

When people today ask "Why Vietnam?" it is obviously *this* involvement and not the very much smaller involvement of two years ago that they have in mind. How shall we answer them now? As we would have two years ago? Or does the quantitative change of the intervening period imply a qualitative change in the nature and implications of American operations in Vietnam?

In seeking answers to these questions, it is perhaps useful to bear in mind that if the United States government had wanted to cut its losses and get out of Vietnam it could have done so with a minimum loss of face and prestige at the time of the final collapse of the Saigon regime around the beginning of 1965. Before then administration spokesmen, including Presidents Eisenhower and Kennedy, had often said that the United States was in South Vietnam to help the government of that country and that in the final analysis it was up to the Vietnamese, not the Americans, to win the war. With the South Vietnamese government knocked out, it would have been perfectly logical—and doubtless would have been well received by world public opinion—to pull out the American "advisers" and call it a day. Moreover, a precedent for such action was ready to hand in the early American reaction to the collapse of Chiang Kai-shek's regime in 1948-1949. No attempt was made at that time to throw in American forces, and the China White Paper of August 1949 was couched in terms which clearly foreshadowed the complete abandonment of Chiang. It was not until the outbreak of the Korean War, nearly a year later, that this policy was reversed.*

It seems reasonable to suppose that there must have been a high-level debate in Washington during the second half of 1964 about whether to pull out or Americanize the war. If we had a record of what went on in this debate—who was on which side and what arguments were advanced in favor of Americanizing the war—we would be able to give a precise answer to the "Why Vietnam?" question. For it is obvious that the crucial decision was made then and that everything that has happened since is in the nature of a logical corollary.

In fact we know very little about what went on behind the scenes in Washington two years ago and must rely on inferences from public statements and actual happenings.

First, then, there is no reason to believe that the original aims of American intervention in Vietnam have been changed, let alone abandoned. Checking the spread of revolution remains the first imperative of United States policy in Asia as elsewhere, and in this respect Vietnam has become more rather than less important. One does not need to believe in any crude version of the domino theory to understand that both revolution and counter-revolution are essentially international—or perhaps better, transnational—phenomena; and that at any given time the attention and energies of both sides tend to be focused on certain key areas where victory or defeat acquires a political and psychological importance which far transcends the local scene. Spain was such an area in the 1930's, and Vietnam is today. As time goes on the Americans become more, not less, anxious to prevent a total victory of the Vietnamese Revolution.

Similarly, the building of an American empire in Southeast Asia, with South Vietnam as its strategic hub, remains a high-priority goal. In this connection what people in the

* For a detailed analysis of American policy in the period immediately following the collapse of the Chiang regime, see "Korea—One Year Later," in *Monthly Review,* August 1951.

West have to understand is that at stake is not some far-distant place of little concern to them but one of the most populous and potentially richest regions of the globe. The land area south of the 17th parallel, east of Burma, and north of Australia contains nearly a million and a half square miles and close to 300 million people. There are only two rivals for possession: revolution and American imperialism. And American imperialism is not about to allow its claim to go by default. Anyone who doubts this should reflect on the meaning of the huge permanent logistical and military installations now being rushed to completion in South Vietnam and Thailand. And anyone who thinks that the leaders of American imperialism have no reason to believe in the possibility of success for their ambitious schemes should reflect on the meaning of last year's bloody preventive counter-revolution which at one blow reduced Indonesia, the richest prize in the whole region, to the status of an abject neo-colony.

It would be a mistake, however, to assume that the reasons for Vietnam today are only what they were when the intervention was first decided upon. Something new and terribly important has been added. As we saw above, the Americanization of the war meant its redirection toward North Vietnam. But North Vietnam is a socialist country, a friend and ally of both the major socialist powers. When the Americans started raining bombs on North Vietnam, they were therefore committing open military aggression against the socialist camp. They did this once before, when MacArthur sought to conquer North Korea in the fall of 1950. That time the reply from the other side was not long in coming: the result was the worst defeat in United States military history. This time the Americans have been more circumspect, confining the aggression to air attacks; and so far there has been no effective reply from the other side.

How long can this situation continue? Will the Americans, emboldened by the absence of retaliation, extend their aggression with the object of further dividing the socialist camp and proving to its weaker members that they cannot rely on protection from the USSR or China? And if the United States does proceed along this tempting course, how will the major socialist powers react and what will be the consequences?

We pose these questions, not with any intent to try to answer them in the present context but rather to point up the fact that a new dimension has been added to the Vietnamese war. It is now not only a counter-revolutionary war and a war for empire, it is also a war between the two world social orders. And the possibility exists that this third war, the war between the systems, may escalate to the point where it swallows up and overwhelms the other two.

We conclude that there is no dearth of reasons for American involvement in Vietnam—reasons which, from the point of view of an aggressively expanding imperialism, are the most compelling imaginable. Blocking revolution on the world's most revolutionary continent—adding great territories and populations to a growing empire—challenging and perhaps seriously weakening the rival world social order—for what other purposes does the United States spend tens of billions of dollars on armaments every year? And where else except in Vietnam can these terrible forces of destruction be brought to bear in furtherance of these aims?

Vietnam and the 1968 Elections

The Johnson administration has been steadily escalating the war in Vietnam since the end of the New Year's bombing pause, and all indications are that further major steps in the same direction will soon be taken. That this is the meaning of Westmoreland's highly publicized return to the United States is taken for granted in Washington. Thus John Herbers reported immediately after Westmoreland's speech to Congress:

There was almost universal agreement among members of Congress today after Gen. William C. Westmoreland's address that the war in Vietnam was likely to be intensified.

Critics of the administration's military policy in Southeast Asia said with resignation that the general's appearance was apparently designed to prepare the way for a greater war. . . .

Senator Fulbright . . . said he believed the administration had brought General Westmoreland on a speaking tour of this country and before Congress as a calculated effort to "pave the way for escalation."

"Developments during the past several weeks, the increased bombings, and other things all point to a much wider war," he said. "The general was preparing the ground for it." . . .

Representative L. Mendel Rivers of South Carolina, chairman of the House Armed Services Committee, said the speech "separates the men from the boys."

"The immortal words of Stephen Decatur, 'my country right or wrong,' could never be truer," he said. "It's too late to question whether it's right or wrong." (*New York Times*, April 29.)

As to the timing of the escalation there seems to be hardly more doubt. Wrote Tom Wicker in his April 27th column in the *New York Times*:

All of this [indications of escalation] can only mean that since the failure to get peace talks under way in January and February, President Johnson has determined on an enormous gamble. He has decided to seek a military decision over North Vietnam on the mainland of Asia, and the probability is that his timetable has been stepped up in an effort to produce an end to the war well before the 1968 election.

In other words, to put it quite baldly, Johnson is now about to gamble tens of thousands of Vietnamese and American lives to improve his electoral chances next year. He wants to regain his popularity, restore his authority in the Democratic Party, and establish a reputation as a great statesman. To do so he must appear before the voters in 1968 as a victor whose political and military judgment has been vindicated.

What are the chances that this strategy will succeed? Close to zero, for two reasons. (1) The war in the South is a revolutionary war which has long since passed the point beyond which it could be "won" by the counter-revolutionary side. And (2) North Vietnam cannot be invaded and occupied (in the sense that South Vietnam now is) without bringing in China and involving the Soviet Union in a much bigger commitment than it has yet made. For either or both reasons, Johnson's hopes of bringing the war to an early end are destined to be disappointed. Let us look at the two points a little more closely.

(1) "Revolutionary warfare," writes Eqbal Ahmad who has both studied it and observed it at first hand in Algeria, "does not require only discontent among the masses but also a sense of desperation and a grim determination to end injustice and humiliation. It demands patience, prolonged suffering, and a determined conspiracy of silence and militancy."* Nowhere have these conditions and qualities been developed to so high a degree as in Vietnam. The purpose of revolutionary war is only partly military; more fundamentally it is to isolate totally the old regime from the masses of the people and simultaneously to begin the construction of a new and just society. Once these objectives have been achieved, no conceivable military effort by

---

* Eqbal Ahmad, "Revolutionary Warfare," in *Alternative Perspectives on Vietnam*: *Report on an International Conference* (The Inter-university Committee for Debate on Foreign Policy, P.O. Box 71, Ithaca, N. Y., $1.00), p. 52. Ahmad's piece is an extraordinarily penetrating and lucid analysis. The *Report* also contains other valuable material, most notably "The Forgotten Element in the Vietnam Discussion: the Facts" by Mortimer Graves, Executive Director Emeritus of the American Council of Learned Societies, which pitilessly exposes the whole tissue of lies which have been concocted to justify the American aggression in Vietnam.

the counter-revolutionary side can restore "law and order"; the most it can achieve is to prolong fighting and prevent the revolution from consolidating its power. In the process, the counter-revolution may win any number of purely military victories; what it cannot do is to bring the past back to life again. "The Algerian revolution," Eqbal Ahmad reminds us, "was actually crushed militarily but had won politically when de Gaulle negotiated independence."* The South Vietnamese revolution won politically as long ago as 1954, as proved again and again by the utter failure of a whole series of "pacification" campaigns by Diem and his successors. Westmoreland, too, will undoubtedly win military victories. What is not conceivable is that he and/or his Vietnamese stooges will be able to end the fighting, still less to govern South Vietnam.

(2) It should be clear by now to everyone with any sense of history that North Vietnam cannot be bombed into surrender. Hanoi and Haiphong and other cities may be razed, as many German and Japanese cities were razed during the Second World War. If so, they will be evacuated, and the North Vietnamese economy and society will be reduced to a subsistence level in the countryside. In the meantime, while bombing from the air yields continuously diminishing returns, its costs will rise as North Vietnam's allies steadily improve the country's air defenses. Since bombing is thus a strategic blind alley, the Johnson administration, in its frantic hunt for quick victory, will be more and more tempted to try an invasion of North Vietnam. If it succumbs to this temptation, the North Vietnamese will obviously have no more reason for not requesting direct Chinese help; and the Chinese will have every reason, both political and military, to meet the request. The United States will then be bogged down in the full-scale war on the Asian mainland against which a long and distinguished succession of military strategists has emphatically warned. There is nothing new in the present situation to make these warnings less relevant now than they have been in the past. No wonder Walter Lippmann cries out in anguish:

---

* *Ibid.*, p. 51.

A measure of how the situation has worsened can be found in some remarks made by Gen. Westmoreland last week [April 9-15]. He said that he knew of no better way to win the war than "to go on bleeding" our adversary. The spectacle of an American commander committed by his government to a war of attrition on the Asian mainland, committed to spending American lives in some exchange ratio against Asian lives, is a startling illustration of what has happened to American military and diplomatic leadership in this war. Imagine Gen. MacArthur, Gen. Eisenhower, Gen. Ridgway, Gen. Bradley, imagine any of the military leaders and thinkers in our history being placed in a position where the defense of freedom on the globe depended on matching American lives against the manpower of Asia!

There are of course those who argue that if China comes into the war, the hands of the United States will then be freed to bomb China. No doubt. But if North Vietnam cannot be bombed into surrender, what reason is there to suppose that China, with its 700 million people dispersed over an area larger than the United States, can be? What General Gavin wrote over a year ago is as true today as it was then: "To increase the bombing and to bomb Hanoi—or even Peking—will add to our problems rather than detract from them."*

Only one conclusion is possible, that short of withdrawal from Vietnam there is no way the United States can end the war in Vietnam this year or next year or at anytime in the foreseeable future. Johnson's strategy is doomed: the chances are that the image he presents to the American voter in 1968 will be that of a mad butcher with nothing but failure to show for his bloody crimes and blunders.

There is of course opposition in the United States ruling class to the Johnson strategy and presumably a growing understanding of where it is leading. How strong is it and what are the chances that it will prevail?

In seeking answers to these questions it will be helpful to review the postwar history of United States policies in Asia. During the first few years after the surrender of Japan there was substantial unity in the American ruling class on Asian policy. The keystone was to be Chiang Kai-shek's China which

---

* "A Communication on Vietnam" from General James M. Gavin, *Harper's Magazine,* February, 1966.

it was hoped to convert into a combination of world's largest and most lucrative neo-colony and junior partner in the control and exploitation of the rest of the Far East. With the collapse of the Chiang regime and the victory of the Chinese Revolution in 1949, this unity in the United States ruling class was shattered.

Two main lines began to emerge almost at once: one advocating a "forward" policy of aid to Chiang Kai-shek and active United States military intervention on the mainland, the other advocating a more moderate "wait-and-see" policy. At the outset the forward group was rather small, consisting mostly of military men and right-wing Republicans. As far as the great majority of the "power elite" was concerned, including its most prestigious generals, the sudden collapse of their entire Asian policy left them in a state of stunned confusion. For the time being, they were content to follow the advice of the State Department's famous China White Paper (compiled under the Secretaryship of Dean Acheson) to "let the dust settle."

This period, which lasted about a year beginning around the middle of 1949, saw a marked decline in the fortunes of Asian reactionaries. The Truman administration publicly disavowed Chiang's regime on Taiwan; the Huk rebels scored successes in the Philippines; Syngman Rhee's position in South Korea rapidly deteriorated. The Asian counter-revolution and its close American allies in the "forward" camp decided that matters were getting desperate and that something would have to be done about it. They therefore cunningly laid a trap in South Korea into which the North Koreans rashly fell. The outbreak of the Korean War altered the balance of forces overnight: the Truman administration invaded the Asian mainland under cover of a UN mandate and simultaneously reversed its policy toward Chiang Kai-shek. Soon after, John Foster Dulles, a right-wing Republican and one of the architects of the Korean War, was commissioned to negotiate a peace treaty with Japan which would lay the basis for a new Washington-Tokyo Axis to take the place of the shattered Washington-Nanking Axis. The "forward" group, now in the ascendancy, proceeded in the fall of 1950 to score its greatest triumph: MacArthur's invasion of North Korea which Truman and the UN were bulldozed into endorsing after it had already been launched.

The Chinese, however, could not be so easily cowed. As MacArthur's troops approached the Yalu River in the winter of 1950-1951, the Chinese struck back hard and the Korean War entered an entirely new phase. So also did the political struggle at home. MacArthur wished to convert his defeat at the hands of the Chinese into an excuse for carrying the war into China. Confronted with this prospect, Truman and his advisers (including Generals Marshall and Bradley) took fright. A dramatic showdown ensued: MacArthur was deliberately insubordinate; Truman fired him; MacArthur came home to appeal over the President's head to the people and their representatives in Congress—and failed.* The drive of the "forward" group was now halted, and Washington reverted once again to a more cautious Asian policy.

The next bid of the "forward" group came with the impending collapse of the French in Indo-China. This time Dulles, now Secretary of State, was the chief organizer and leader; within the government he was backed by such powerful figures as Vice President Nixon and Admiral Radford (Chairman of the Joint Chiefs of Staff). Their plan was to intervene militarily on behalf of the French, knowing full well that this would soon mean taking over the war entirely. (Washington was already paying something like four fifths of the cost of the French effort in Indo-China, and the political situation in France was such that withdrawal of French troops was mandatory on any government hoping to remain in power.) But President Eisenhower, on the urgent advice of the Army, refused to go along; as in 1951, the "forward" group was once again defeated. It is worth recalling today what General Matthew B. Ridgway, then Army Chief of Staff, said about this episode in his memoirs:

In Korea we had learned that air and naval power alone cannot win a war and that inadequate ground forces cannot win one either. It was incredible to me that we had forgotten that bitter lesson so soon—that we were on the verge of making the same tragic error.

---

* Later, after his retirement, MacArthur strongly advised against getting into a land war against China.

That error, thank God, was not repeated. . . . The idea of intervention was abandoned, and it is my belief that the analysis which the Army made and presented to higher authority played a considerable, perhaps a decisive, part in persuading our government not to embark on that tragic adventure.

Following his failure to achieve military intervention on the Asian mainland in 1954, Dulles found it necessary to resort to more cautious and devious methods of achieving his aims in Asia.* One key move was to conclude a military alliance with Chiang Kai-shek's regime on Taiwan, an arrangement which, as long as it existed, was guaranteed to make impossible any rapprochement between the United States and China. And another step was to construct, in the same year of 1954, the Southeast Asia Treaty Organization (SEATO) which brought three Asian countries (Pakistan, Thailand, and the Philippines) directly under the American military wing and was drafted in such a way as to give the United States the semblance of an international mandate to "protect" the independent successor states to French Indo-China (Laos, Cambodia, and Vietnam) which had been agreed to at the Geneva Conference of 1954.

As to Indo-China itself, Dulles's strategy was to set up a separate puppet state in South Vietnam—in clear violation of the Geneva Agreements which solemnly affirmed the unity of Vietnam and which the United States had publicly stated its intention not to subvert. His calculation was that a regime similar to that of Syngman Rhee in South Korea could be established

---

* About the aims as such there was neither any mystery nor any dispute within the ruling class. They were succinctly set forth in testimony by Walter S. Robertson, Dulles's Assistant Secretary of State for Far Eastern Affairs, at a hearing before the House Appropriations Committee on January 26, 1954. The questions are by Representative Frederic R. Coudert, the answers by Robertson:

"*Q*. Did I correctly understand you to say that the heart of the present policy toward China and Formosa is that there is to be kept alive a constant threat of military action vis-à-vis Red China in the hope that at some point there will be an internal breakdown?

"*A*. Yes, sir, that is my conception.

"*Q*. Fundamentally, does that not mean that the United States is undertaking to maintain for an indefinite period of years American dominance in the Far East?

"*A*. Yes. Exactly." (Quoted in Edgar Snow, *The Other Side of the River*, p. 631.)

in South Vietnam and maintained in power by liberal hand-outs of military and economic assistance. This would erect a barrier to the spread of communism (i.e. revolution) and make possible the consolidation of United States control over the whole area of Southeast Asia. That this was the real goal of American policy had been clearly indicated by President Eisenhower when, as reported in the *New York Times* of August 5, 1953, he told a conference of state governors that "losing" Indo-China would be "of most terrible significance to the United States of America, our security, our power and ability to get things we need from the riches of . . . Southeast Asia."

At the time there was no significant opposition to this policy in the American ruling class, any more than there had been to propping up and relying on Chiang Kai-shek at the end of the Second World War. And yet in the one case as in the other, failure was inevitable, and for the same reason. The revolutionary process had already passed beyond the point of no return in Vietnam: the Vietnamese people had become quite literally ungovernable by a regime of domestic and foreign exploiters. This truth of course did not emerge into the light of day all at once; in fact, it was a full decade before the puppet state finally collapsed. During this period the steady weakening of the regime of Ngo Dinh Diem and his successors could be lied about, its failures denied or explained away; and ever new promises of success just around the corner could be issued in Washington and Saigon.* But the hour of truth could not be delayed forever: by mid-1964 the puppet armies had been defeated in battle or were melting away; like ripe fruit, power was about to fall into the outstretched hands of the National Liberation Front.

The hour of truth in Vietnam was the hour of decision in Washington. Once again, as in 1954, the United States had to choose between accepting what had actually happened on the field of battle and throwing in its own forces in an attempt to

---

* On this, see the review article by Hugh Deane, "The Permanent Promise: A Critique of the Liberal Books on Vietnam," in *Monthly Review*, June 1967.

reverse the military verdict. And this time, unlike in 1954, the decision was made to Americanize the war.

It is not clear when this decision was made, but it was almost certainly before the Tonkin Gulf incident of August 4, 1964, which was obviously cooked up by the Pentagon and used by Johnson as a pretext for getting the Congress to pass a Joint Resolution that Senator Morse, speaking on the Senate floor on August 5th, correctly labelled a "predated declaration of war."

Was there any opposition within the administration to this decision? If so, it has never been publicized and it cannot have been very significant. In 1954, the Army of which General Ridgway was then 'Chief of Staff, had, as we have already noted, strongly opposed the "forward" policy. This time, with one Army officer Chief of Staff of the Army and another Army officer occupying the highest military position as Chairman of the Joint Chiefs, there was apparently no such opposition. And Johnson, unlike Truman in 1952 and Eisenhower in 1954, joined the "forward" camp (when the facts are known, it may even turn out that he was its leader). Even in the Senate the opposition to the "predated declaration of war" was extremely feeble and did *not* include Senator Fulbright, the Chairman of the Foreign Relations Committee, who has since become the leading Senatorial critic of the policy of escalation.

Nor is there any reason to believe that strong opposition existed in ruling-class circles outside the government. Has this situation significantly changed in the last two and a half years of steady escalation? If so, there is not much evidence of it. The circle of Senatorial critics has increased somewhat but remains small. No prestigious military figures have joined Generals Gavin and Ridgway in warning of the perils of an expanded war on the Asian mainland. Walter Lippmann remains a pretty lonely figure in the journalistic world, though occasionally *New York Times* columnists James Reston and Tom Wicker sound as though they would like to do more than merely raise questions. One hears stories about opposition to the war in business circles, especially, it is said, among East Coast financiers; we have no reason to doubt that such opposition exists, but so far at any rate it has been too discreet and private to give any clues to its size and intensity. As far as the public record goes, one can only conclude that the American ruling class in general approves of Johnson's war policy.

One can go further and say that even those elements in the ruling class which do not approve are either unwilling or unable to propose an alternative that has any better chance of succeeding (success of course being judged from a ruling-class point of view). The only way to end the war, we repeat, is for the United States to withdraw and leave Vietnam to the Vietnamese. Unless and until that happens, or at least is promised in terms that satisfy a people who have been grossly deceived and cheated by promises before, the fighting will go on. And yet Senator McGovern, in a recent Senate speech in which he eloquently pictured the horror and the hopelessness of the Johnson course, felt it necessary to emphasize that not a single Senatorial critic of the war had ever advocated United States withdrawal.

It is against this background that one must evaluate the prospect, now much under discussion, that the Republicans will run an antiwar candidate in 1968. We do not question that the possibility of such a candidacy exists or that it would stand a good chance of electoral success. The war in Vietnam is unpopular and getting more so, and Johnson's political fortunes are indissolubly tied to it. He will be relatively easy to beat next year, and a peace candidate would probably have the best chance of turning the trick. The Republican Party is of course well aware of this state of affairs and is making preparations to capitalize on it (as, for example, in the well publicized "Blue Book" on Vietnam issued by the Senate Republican Policy Committee on May 1), while a number of aspiring candidates—most notably Senator Percy of Illinois and Mayor Lindsay of New York—are seeking to establish reputations as opponents of the war.

What is not clear, however, is whether a Republican in the White House, no matter what platform he might be elected on, would make much difference. Remember that Johnson ran as a peace candidate in 1964 and promptly escalated the war. The explanation, put in its simplest form, is that the military-industrial complex in Washington and across the country wanted a bigger war and no significant element of the ruling class was seriously opposed. If this situation had really changed, a Republican President might be able to de-escalate and at least explore the possibilities of finding some acceptable way to withdraw from Vietnam. But if, as our analysis above seems to indicate, there has been no significant shift in the balance of forces within the ruling class, a peace candidacy in 1968 will mean no more than Johnson's peace candidacy did in 1964.

Of course things may change in a way to put the 1968 election in a different light. Once before, in 1951-1952, the advocates of the "forward" policy in Asia were riding high and yet were unable to achieve what was then their major goal, the extension of the Korean War into China. Paradoxically, what frustrated their drive was determined military action by the Chinese. A comparable situation could arise in Vietnam if the Johnson administration decides to invade the North. Confronted again by the reality of a land war with China, a powerful part of the ruling class might wish to draw back, as it did in 1952. In that case the 1968 election might become the arena for resolving a genuine struggle within the ruling class.

However that may be, it seems crystal clear to us that those who are really for peace, and not simply against wars the United States may lose, should steer scrupulously clear of ruling-class electoral politics. The whole history of the postwar period irrefutably proves that no section of the American ruling class is opposed to the imposition of United States domination on the largest possible part of the world: they differ only on the definition of "largest possible" at any given time. And if, what now seems highly unlikely, a group favoring withdrawal from Vietnam should get into power, its purpose would only be to conserve American power for more effective use elsewhere against people struggling for liberation and the right to decide their own destinies.

A peace movement worthy of the name in the United States must take its place at the side of these struggling peoples and not line up with this or that faction of the ruling class every time an election comes around. And while it must agitate against—

and educate around—every war, its deeper purpose must be to change the character of the United States from the war-making imperialist aggressor it now is to a genuinely peaceful nation respecting the right of other nations to shape their own future.

In the long run, this deeper purpose can be achieved only by a profound social revolution, a fact which the new radicalism of the 1960's is coming to understand. But that does not mean that nothing can be done now. Until we can change the system, our primary aim must be to weaken it, to reduce as much as possible its capacity to fight wars of aggression against other peoples. And that in turn means doing everything possible to deprive it of the military manpower without which all its vaunted planes and bombs and guns are so much junk.

The really effective peace movement today is much smaller than the hundreds of thousands of demonstrators who marched in New York and San Francisco on April 15th. But its potential is much greater. It consists in the first instance of those who bravely defy the draft or refuse to go to Vietnam, and behind them of those who in various ways encourage these acts of defiance and resistance. As of now the outstanding figures are Muhammad Ali, Stokely Carmichael, and Martin Luther King, Jr. It is no accident that they are all blacks, for United States imperialism not only oppresses and exploits black Americans but cynically uses them as mercenaries to oppress and exploit people of color all over the world.

As to the potential power of this still-small movement of resistance to military service, it will be enough to quote from two recent columns in the *New York Times*. The first appeared on May 2 under the title "In the Nation: Muhammad Ali and Dissent" and is by Tom Wicker. Raising the question, "if large numbers of these dissenters simply refused military service, what could the government of a democracy do?" Wicker proceeds:

A hundred thousand Muhammad Alis, of course, could be jailed. But if the Johnson administration had to prosecute 100,000 Americans in order to maintain its authority, its real power to pursue the Vietnamese war or any other policy would be crippled if not destroyed. It would then be faced not with dissent but with civil disobedience on a scale amounting to revolt.

Is there any chance that a resistance movement of such magnitude may develop? Perhaps Reston's column of May 5th ("Washington: Compromise on the Military Draft") gives us a clue to an answer. According to Reston, one of the reasons why the Senate Armed Services Committee shied away from advocating the ending of undergraduate draft deferments is that "it might inflame opposition on the university campuses into a national crisis." He then goes on:

Officials discuss this latter point very cautiously, but it is a factor. The opposition in the universities to the Vietnam war is already an embarrassment and an irritation to the administration. But there is genuine fear here [Washington] that abolition of all or most college deferments might lead to massive defiance among undergraduates. One estimate here is that if college students were called like any other nineteen-year-olds, as many as 25 percent might refuse to serve.

Washington's fears may be exaggerated, but whether or not that is the case they point very clearly to the Achilles Heel of American imperialism. And they give us the right to hope that the United States may yet develop the most effective peace movement of our time.

The Fall of McNamara

Why was McNamara kicked downstairs to the presidency of the World Bank? And what does it mean?

There is little doubt about the answer to the first question: McNamara was having increasing doubts about the war in Vietnam. To cite the apparently well-informed account in *Newsweek* (December 11):

For all his public support of the Johnson war policy . . . , McNamara's doubts about the conduct of the war are a familiar story to his liberal admirers. One friend remembers a conversation in which McNamara expressed haunting fears that his counsel to two Presidents to pursue the war may have been ill-advised. Last spring, according to another friend, Bob McNamara's wife "Marg" took him aside at a party to report that her husband was so at war with himself that they had been up until 4 a.m. discussing whether he should resign. Later in the evening, McNamara himself repeated the story. He felt, he said, that it was about time to bow out.

Little goes on in Washington that Lyndon Johnson doesn't hear about—and McNamara's self-doubts were no secret at the White House. Increasingly in recent weeks, one source says, the President began to complain that McNamara was telling him one thing and Georgetown friends something else. Others report that Mr. Johnson lately referred sarcastically to his Defense Secretary as "that military genius" and that he complained to a visiting Senator: "McNamara's gone dovish on me."

Under these circumstances it was obviously smarter from Johnson's point of view to get rid of McNamara on the best available pretext rather than run the risk that the Secretary would resign at a politically embarrassing moment.

As to the meaning of McNamara's departure from the Pentagon, there is widespread agreement among knowledgeable observers. Reports Alvin Shuster from London in the *New York Times* of November 29th:

The pending departure of Robert S. McNamara as United States Secretary of Defense has raised fears in European capitals that the administration plans a more adventuresome policy of escalation of the war in Vietnam. . . .

The main thrust of the reactions was that the Joint Chiefs of Staff had won out in a struggle for an escalated war and that Mr. McNamara was being moved out to make it possible. . . .

In Paris, officials and bankers took the view that the McNamara shift was one more indication that "rational views within the administration are losing out."

In Rome, those interviewed said that the Secretary was admired as one of the "last holdovers from the popular Kennedy administration and for his reputation for having established firm civilian control over the generals and admirals." They regarded his departure as opening the door for escalation of the war.

Similar views have been expressed by both right-wing and left-wing observers in the United States. According to Evans and Novak in their syndicated column of November 30th, "the reasons underlying McNamara's departure show that this is a time when the views of the military, not Pentagon civilians, are pre-eminent." And I. F. Stone states flatly: "Worse certainly lies ahead. I believe McNamara's going signals escalation." (*I. F. Stone's Weekly*, December 4.)

There is no reason that we know of to dispute this interpretation. But it does imply a paradox which should be recognized and if possible explained. No individual has been more closely identified with and responsible for the war in Vietnam than McNamara, as evidenced by the fact that it has often been called "McNamara's War." How does it happen that now, at a time of maximum United States involvement, this super-advocate and chief organizer develops doubts and misgivings of such a serious nature that the Johnson administration no longer dares to count on his continued loyal support?

In seeking an answer to this question we have to take into account McNamara's background and qualifications. He graduated from the University of California at Berkeley in the mid-1930's and went on to the Harvard Business School where he made such a favorable impression that he was immediately appointed to the faculty. During the Second World War he entered the Air Force, rising rapidly and while still under the age of 30 to the rank of Lieutenant Colonel. There he was instrumental in introducing new management techniques. In 1946 he and a number of young associates, soon to be known as the "Whiz Kids," sold themselves as a group to the highest bidder, which happened to be the Ford Motor Company, then in bad shape and much in need of a managerial blood transfusion. At Ford, McNamara's rise was uninterrupted; and by the time Kennedy appointed him Secretary of Defense in 1960 he had attained the company's presidency, one of the highest positions in the United States corporate elite which in turn constitutes the leading echelon of the American ruling class.

Kennedy's choice was a logical one: McNamara was in every way an exemplary leader and spokesman for this class. Possessed of a brilliant intellect, trained in the country's most prestigious educational institutions, a proven success in both segments of the military-industrial complex, he was also a near-perfect embodiment of the values and aspirations of a "liberal imperialist" society. In commenting on his appointment to the World Bank, *Newsweek* (December 11) wrote: "For all his public identification with missiles and megadeath estimates, he is a humanist with an abiding concern for the kind of work the World Bank does in underdeveloped nations. He expressed that concern in a celebrated speech in Montreal in May 1966— tying global stability to the plight of the have-not nations."

The Montreal speech is indeed justly celebrated: it expresses perhaps more clearly than any statement of recent years the rationale of United States world policy.

The central theme of the Montreal speech is what purports to be a theory of violence in the modern world and how to reduce or eliminate it—surely a worthy and humane purpose. "In the last eight years alone," McNamara told his audience of newspaper editors, "there have been no less than 164 internationally significant outbreaks of violence—each of them specifically designed as a serious challenge to the authority, or the very existence, of the government in question." And he went on to present statistics to show that the trend of such conflicts is upward (wherefore "the planet is becoming a more dangerous place to live on"); that there is a strong positive correlation between the poverty of a country (as measured by its per capita income) and the likelihood of its being involved in such violence; and that the gap between the rich nations and the poor nations is widening. Since most of the poorest, and hence most violence-prone, nations are in the southern hemisphere, "The conclusion of all this is blunt and inescapable: Given the certain connection between economic stagnation and the incidence of violence, the years that lie ahead for the nations in the southern half of the globe are pregnant with violence." Further: "Whether Communists are involved or not, violence transmits sharp signals through the complex ganglia of international relations; and the security of the United States is related to the security and stability of nations half a globe away." (Quotations are from the *New York Times* of May 19, 1966.) From this reasoning there follows a prescription for United States security (which McNamara treats as the self-evident, overriding goal of national policy): Help the poor countries to develop so that they can become stable and secure from violence, and in the meantime provide them with military protection against aggression or subversion which could prevent or interrupt what he calls the "modernization process."

It should be noted that in this view violence is not blamed on Communism: Communists, according to McNamara, merely take advantage of the natural and justified frustration and anger of the poor. The United States can therefore assure its own security not by a war on Communism but by a global war on poverty. National interest and humanitarianism therefore coincide: whatever is done to promote the one automatically promotes the other.

Liberals were of course enchanted with the Montreal speech—with its apparent abhorrence of violence, its espousal of generous United States aid to "modernizing" countries, and its deliberate playing down of the Communist menace. A radical, on the other hand, should have no trouble in seeing through the liberal phraseology to the hard-line counter-revolutionary core of McNamara's thought. The crux of the matter is that he singles out only one form of violence in the poor countries, that directed against governments, and totally neglects the infinitely more widespread and intensive forms of violence which are built into the very fabric of these societies. What about the violence that keeps landless peasants and slum-dwellers at literally starvation levels while small oligarchies live in air-conditioned luxury? Is it not violence, immediate and naked, when, in one of the potentially wealthiest countries in the world, a population of some 20 million has the following character-istics: illiteracy—over 70 percent; caloric intake—between 1200 and 1900 per day; incidence of schistosomiasis—90 percent; incidence of intestinal parasites—over 90 percent?*

The truth is that McNamara condones the ubiquitous violence of the status quo and condemns only the selective and, by comparison, miniscule violence directed at changing the status quo. The rising trend of the latter form of violence, far from being a bad thing, is the most hopeful development of our time: it shows that the wretched of the earth have had enough and that from now on violence will be increasingly used to liquidate exploitation rather than perpetuate it. And *this* is what alarms the chief architect of the greatest violence-making ma-chine in history.

It is against this background that one must assess McNa-mara's role at the Pentagon. He assumed office as Secretary of Defense with two missions, one minor and one major. The minor mission was to reorganize the Department along lines indicated by the latest management theories. The major mis-sion was vastly to expand the size, striking power, and flexibility of the whole military establishment. With the enthusiastic back-ing of the new President and close to $50 billion to spend, McNamara seems to have undertaken his assignment with no doubts about the practical omnipotence of American power. When the Southeast Asian policy of the Kennedy administra-tion was being shaped in the Laos crises of 1961 and 1962, McNamara generally ranged himself alongside the Joint Chiefs of Staff in favor of military solutions. And the same was true as attention shifted increasingly to Vietnam. How, then, are

---

* The area is Northeast Brazil and the figures are from a recent report distributed by the Institute of Current World Affairs. Comparable conditions exist throughout the poorer countries—and even in parts of the richer countries, such as Mississippi and Appalachia in the United States itself.

we to explain the later break with the generals which led to his downfall?*

Part of the answer seems to be that until fairly recently McNamara really believed in the possibility of winning a war of limited intervention in Southeast Asia. There is considerable evidence for this in Hilsman's book. For example, Hilsman reports on a strategy meeting in Honolulu which he attended as Assistant Secretary of State for Far Eastern Affairs in April, 1963:

General Harkins [then United States commander in Saigon] gave us all the facts and figures—the number of strategic hamlets established, number of Viet Cong killed, operations initiated by government forces, and so on. He could not of course, he said, give any guarantees, but he thought he could say by Christmas it would be all over. The Secretary of Defense was elated. He reminded me that I had attended one of the very first of these meetings, when it had all looked so black—and that had been only a year and a half ago. (pp. 466-467)

Events of course took a different turn from that predicted by General Harkins. In the summer and fall of 1963 there occurred the first great Buddhist crisis and the overthrow of the Diem regime in Saigon. In the midst of this turmoil, McNamara and General Maxwell Taylor flew to Vietnam "to get the facts." On their return, according to Hilsman's account:

McNamara and Taylor had come a long way in recognizing that political factors were more important in Vietnam than they had been willing to admit, but they had not come far enough to recognize that political factors were fundamental and overriding. They still really believed that the war was being won. They still really believed that military measures would suffice. And they still really believed in statistics. . . . Their proposal was implicit rather than explicit, but it was clear. McNamara and the Joint Chiefs would agree to a policy of "pressure and persuasion" on the Diem regime, which they now thought was necessary, but they would agree only if the White House and the State Department

---

* The most revealing source we know of on this whole range of subjects is the book of Roger Hilsman, *To Move a Nation: The Politics of Foreign Policy in the Administration of John F. Kennedy*, New York 1967. Hilsman held high positions in the Kennedy administration and resigned from the State Department because of policy disagreements two months after Johnson came to power.

would in turn agree to a public announcement that the Pentagon was right about how the "shooting war" had been going. McNamara's tone, when he read the proposed language of the announcement to the NSC on his return October 2, was almost brusque, as if he were delivering an ultimatum:

"The military program in South Vietnam has made progress and is sound in principle, though improvements are being energetically sought. . . .

"Secretary McNamara and General Taylor reported their judgment that the major part of the United States military task can be completed by the end of 1965. . . ." (p. 510)

The statement was made public immediately after the meeting; and, as Hilsman says, it "came to haunt Secretary McNamara and the whole history of American involvement in Vietnam." (p. 511.) It is simply incredible that McNamara would have stuck his neck out this way if he had not believed in the substantial accuracy of the statement.

But this still does not explain the break with the military. They too may have believed in the possibility of winning a limited war of intervention. What they did *not* believe in—and this was apparently the main difference between them and McNamara—was the desirability of keeping it a limited war. One of the most important contributions of Hilsman's book is its authoritative revelation of military thinking on this possibly crucially important point. After explaining that "to many of the higher-ranking American military, the Korean War was a frustrating humiliation," Hilsman goes on to state that

by 1961 it was a shibboleth among the Joint Chiefs of Staff that the United States ought never again to fight a limited war on the ground in Asia or perhaps never again to fight any kind of war on the ground in Asia. So often was the view expressed, in fact, that people in Washington began to speak of the "Never Again" Club. . . . The general thrust of their memoranda seemed to imply that they were demanding an advance commitment from the President that, if they agreed to the use of American force and there were any fighting at all, then there would be no holds barred whatsoever—including the use of nuclear weapons. (p. 129)

This was written in connection with the Laos crisis of 1961. As time went on, the "Never Again" attitude hardened, with the significant difference that as American forces became increasingly involved in the fighting in Vietnam its meaning gradually narrowed down to "never again fight a *limited* war on the ground in Asia." In the light of what we now know, we can take Hanson Baldwin's famous article in the *New York Times Magazine* of February 21, 1965, as a sort of public declaration of the new strategic doctrine, supplanting what had long been conventional military wisdom to avoid committing United States forces to a ground war on the Asian mainland. At the time we speculated that this might be the meaning of the article. Noting that in the past it had always been the Army which had been the chief opponent of getting involved in an Asian ground war, we wrote:

There is now reason to believe that this opposition on the part of the Army has been modified and perhaps abandoned altogether. Most important in this connection is the article by Hanson W. Baldwin in the *New York Times Magazine* of February 21st, advocating a vastly increased commitment of American forces [up to a million men] to the war in Vietnam. . . . Baldwin, the paper's military editor, is known to have close connections in the Pentagon and has not acquired the reputation of being a spokesman for only one of the services. While one cannot be certain, it nevertheless seems likely that Baldwin's advocacy of an all-out effort reflects the views of all three services.*

We can now be certain: *the United States military wants an unlimited war on the Asian mainland.*

We do not know when McNamara began to have doubts about the possibility of winning a limited war in Vietnam; but once he did, it was logical that he should part company with the professional military people. He is a business man, not a fighting man. Not only has he brought business methods into the Pentagon but, more important, he sees the military machine as the instrument of the socio-economic system, to be used in furtherance of the interests of the beneficiaries of the system. This is the traditional view of the American bourgeoisie, enshrined in the constitutional provision for civilian control over the armed forces; and it accurately reflects the way American capitalism has functioned on the world stage since the founding of the Republic. In this sense McNamara is simply a traditionalist. To account for his break with the generals and admirals, we need only credit him with the capacity to understand that

---

* See above, pp. 43–59.

an unlimited war on the Asian mainland, far from being in the interests of the American Empire is the clearly marked road to Decline and Fall.

As this analysis implies, what is new in the present situation is the emergence as an important force in American society of militarism in the classic sense, that is to say, of a group of professional military commanders who see the military establishment not merely as the servitor of capitalist-imperialist interests but also as an autonomous entity with a life and goals of its own. For the most part, of course, there have been no serious conflicts in the postwar period between capitalist-imperialist interests and the goals of the militarist faction, a fact which has permitted the latter to grow to its present dimensions and strength almost unnoticed. But now the militarists' goals have come to encompass the fighting and presumably in some sense the winning of an unlimited war of conquest on the Asian mainland. We do not pretend to be able to give a full explanation of this development, but some of the factors at work are fairly clear. There is the desire to use to the full the huge engine of destruction which has been built up since the demobilization following the Second World War; and since attacking the Soviet Union would be risking nuclear annihilation, Asia is the only suitable theater. There is the thirst for revenge for the "defeat" in the Korean War.* There is the feeling, shared by many non-militarists, that sooner or later war with China is inevitable anyway and that it may be better that it should come sooner rather than later. And finally there is a certain hankering for the enhanced power and prestige which inevitably accrue to the military in an all-out war situation.

Civilian bourgeois leaders like McNamara have no interest in using the war machine simply because it exists, and they obviously do not want to lose real power to the military. But an even more important reason for their rejecting the idea of an unlimited Asian war is their awareness of the global char-

---

* In this there is a strong element of racism, clearly hinted at in Hilsman's comment on the sense of humiliation caused by Korea: "The American Army had been fought to a standstill by Asians, and by Asians whose arms and equipment were somewhat primitive by American standards." (p. 128)

acter of American interests. All-out involvement in East and
Southeast Asia means all-out weakness in South and West Asia,
Africa, Europe, and Latin America. Rival imperialists and ever-
growing numbers of revolutionaries in the underdeveloped countries are ready and eager to dismember the American Empire,
piece by piece or all at once, if and when the United States
gets hopelessly bogged down in a widespread and protracted
war on the Asian mainland. It was undoubtedly this more than
anything else which played an increasingly determining role in
McNamara's thinking as the mirage of victory in a limited war
receded into the background.

What about Johnson's role in all this?

To begin with, it is important to recognize that he has been
one of the most extreme hawks on Vietnam from the very beginning. As Vice President, he was sent in May 1961, by Kennedy on a tour of Asian countries, in the course of which he
hailed Diem as the Churchill of Southeast Asia. On his return
home, according to Hilsman, "the Vice President recommended
a fundamental decision to 'move forward promptly with a major
effort to help these countries defend themselves.' Time was
running out, he felt, and the United States had to 'pull back
our defenses to San Francisco and a "Fortress America" concept' or go ahead with a full, forward strategy." (p. 422) A
few months later General Maxwell Taylor headed a mission to
Vietnam which recommended, among other things, "the introduction into Vietnam of over ten thousand regular American
ground troops, initially, and accepting the possibility that as
many as six full divisions might eventually be required." This
was "essentially the same large-scale commitment that Vice
President Johnson had recommended"; and several sentences
later, Hilsman speaks of the "Taylor-Johnson policy." (p. 423)
Except in public speeches during the 1964 election campaign,
Johnson continued to hew to this Pentagonian line on Vietnam; and the firing of McNamara shows that if he has had any
second thoughts, he has not shown any disposition to act on
them. For it is clear that if he had wanted to resist the generals,
McNamara would have been his most valuable ally.

How can we explain that Johnson, a civilian and always
a faithful servitor of the corporate establishment, now seems to

be moving with the militarists toward an all-out war on the Asian mainland? Partly, perhaps, because he believes the nonsense put out by Westmoreland, Bunker et al that the war is going well for the United States: in other words, he may still not have lost his faith in the possibility which McNamara also used to believe in, that victory can be won in a limited war. Partly no doubt because at heart he is the kind of small-town chauvinist who easily succumbs to militarism. But most likely the main reason is that he is caught in a political trap from which there is quite literally no escape. He cannot now go before the people and say that the whole escalation policy for which he has been responsible these last four years has been a ghastly mistake. And he cannot bring the situation in Vietnam under control. Under the circumstances, he gives in to the military a little at a time and hopes for a miracle.

Where this is leading is perfectly clear: to a victory for the military and an all-out war on the Asian mainland, involving China certainly and possibly the Soviet Union as well. The other side of the coin, as we have already noted, will be the weakening and break-up of the American Empire in other parts of the world. At home all existing tensions and contradictions will be vastly intensified and many new ones created, with consequences which boggle the imagination.

One can only conclude that the downfall of the American Empire and the end of United States capitalism may be much closer at hand than we have been accustomed to think. It will be at best a frightful process, but one cannot deny at any rate that these monstrous social formations deserve the fate which now threatens them, and that their destruction would at least make it possible for mankind to reconstruct in peace. Perhaps on a very long view of history it is better that it should be so.

Events may still take another course, to be sure. There are undoubtedly many members of the ruling class who are at least dimly aware of where the country is now headed. "It is difficult to conceive, personally," writes George F. Kennan in the Autumn 1967, issue of *Harvard Today*, "of any outcome of our present efforts and approaches that would be less than disastrous." The departure of Robert S. McNamara from the Pentagon will doubtless cause others to take alarm. He was, as we noted earlier, the very embodiment of the qualities which the American bourgeoisie holds in highest esteem. As long as he remained at the helm in the Pentagon and assured the nation that all was going well, there must have been many, especially in the corporate elite, who were willing to put aside their doubts and take his assurances at face value. What will they think now? And more important, what will they do now? Will they attempt to make use of the opportunity offered by the 1968 election to replace Johnson with a Republican who might be pledged, at least behind the scenes, to fight to restore civilian supremacy over the military, which of course would necessarily involve withdrawing American forces from Vietnam?

We do not know. We do not even know whether a fight to restore civilian supremacy could now be successful: the militarists may already be firmly in the saddle and able to control *any* president who may be elected. After all, we have no de Gaulles in this country, and the institutional machinery for asserting control over the Pentagon and its allies in the CIA and the armaments industries is, to say the least, weak and untested. As of now, at any rate, the odds would seem to favor victory for those who favor plunging ahead into the great Asian adventure.

In conclusion, we can only add what we have said in these pages before. We in the radical and peace movements are not going to be able to decide the outcome of conflicts and struggles in the United States ruling class now or in the near future. It is better we should not get mixed up in them but rather should concentrate our limited resources and energies on educating, through words and deeds, as large a part of the American people as possible to the true nature of the system under which they live. To understand it is to understand the necessity to get rid of it.

Prospects for Peace, Foreign and Domestic

More than two years ago we predicted that "the number one casualty of the Vietnamese war is going to be Lyndon B. Johnson."* This has now been confirmed, sooner than we expected, by none other than Mr. Johnson himself. With his Gallup poll rating at its lowest point since he became President, unable (in the words of James Reston) to "venture openly into any of the great cities of the United States without the risk of serious demonstrations against him," having (according to Evans and Novak) "reached a nadir of popular support unprecedented for White House incumbents in this century," Lyndon B. Johnson decided to call it quits before he could be further humiliated by his own Party or by the electorate.

At first it seemed that the March 31st speech, coupling announcement of a partial bombing halt with the statement of withdrawal from the presidential race, might be a typical piece of Johnson trickery. Since Hanoi had repeatedly said that it would not enter any talks until *all* bombing of North Vietnam had been stopped, it appeared that Johnson was setting up a situation in which he could (1) claim that his peace overtures had been rejected, (2) escalate the war, (3) put the country on a full war footing, and (4) remain in power — with or without an election — as an indispensable wartime leader.

Such may well have been the plot, and it is perhaps too early to write it off as completely unrealistic. Still, with each passing day it seems less and less likely that events will conform to this script. In a tactical shift, Hanoi agreed to talk — not about peace, to be sure, but for the time being the political effect was pretty much the same. But undoubtedly more important is the increasingly obvious fact that Johnson was so thoroughly discredited that even the hawks would find his leader-

---

* *Monthly Review*, March 1966; included as Chapter 4 of this volume.

ship a possibly fatal liability. Such is the fruit of four years of unrelieved failure, culminating in the worst defeat the United States has suffered in its entire history.

To say this is of course not to subscribe to the theory of individual responsibility for great historic trends and events. The political directorate of the American ruling class, with very few dissenters, approved and supported the involvement of the United States in Vietnam, beginning some two decades ago and steadily increasing under both Republican and Democratic administrations. The aims and motives were those normal to an imperialist power; the strategy was based on the assumption that the United States, being incomparably richer and better supplied with arms, could impose its will on the Vietnamese people. Lyndon B. Johnson just had the bad luck to be in charge of the enterprise when this assumption was finally proved false. If John F. Kennedy had lived and been re-elected in 1964, the failure and ignominy would no doubt have been his: an assassin's bullet preserved for him a brighter niche in the annals of American history.

Is Peace in Sight?

Does the fall of Johnson portend an early peace in Vietnam? Many people, perhaps especially on the Left, seem to assume that it does. The reasoning is that the United States has been defeated on the battlefield, that this fact is now all but universally recognized and admitted, and that the American government — under Johnson or whoever succeeds him — now has no alternative to pulling out of Vietnam while saving as much face as possible. The matter was stated very bluntly by the *Wall Street Journal* in an editorial entitled "The Logic of the Battlefield" (February 23, 1968):

We think the American people should be getting ready to accept, if they haven't already, the prospect that the whole Vietnam effort may be doomed; it may be falling apart beneath our feet. . . .
Hanoi is believed to have relatively large numbers of troops still uncommitted in North Vietnam. The Communists appear to be getting ample supplies of weapons from the Soviet Union and Red China. As long as the arms keep coming and there are Vietnamese Communists to use them, you would suppose that they could keep up the struggle more or less indefinitely. Thus far, at

least, they are showing with a vengeance their ability to sow destruction and demoralization everywhere.

Meantime, the present South Vietnamese government, never very impressive, looks worse and worse. Most important, the government can't protect the people even in the heart of the cities. . . . This is a government and a nation in chaos; how long can it go on?

The U.S. went in to keep South Vietnam out of Communist hands. But no matter what our forces do, they can't seem to do that. If practically nothing is to be left of government or nation, what is there to be saved for what?

The U.S. also went in to demonstrate to Communist China that it couldn't get away with this kind of indirect aggression and that it hadn't better try direct aggression either. But the Communists are getting away with it; they are putting the mighty U.S. through a wringer, and they may be encouraged to try more of it . . .

Conceivably all this is wrong; conceivably the Communists are on the brink of defeat and genuine peace talks are about to begin. It doesn't look that way, and as long as it doesn't everyone had better be prepared for the bitter taste of defeat beyond America's power to prevent.

Perhaps even more striking is a strong editorial statement by *Business Week,* a McGraw-Hill publication which until recently was a complacently uncritical supporter of United States policies in Southeast Asia. The editorial, entitled "A New Policy for Vietnam" and published before Johnson's speech (in the issue dated March 31), reads in part:

In taking these steps [refusal to send 206,000 additional troops to Vietnam and relieving Westmoreland of his command there], the President seems to be facing up to the fact that the long process of escalation has failed to break the strength of the Vietcong and the North Vietnamese — and that there is scant reason to hope that the tide could be turned by sending even the full 206,000 troops Westmoreland called for. This is a war in which the U.S. has consistently underestimated the enemy's strength and determination. A decisive military victory cannot be achieved with anything less than a massive new buildup of troops and arms in South Vietnam and an invasion of North Vietnam.

Certainly there is a sizable group of Americans who feel that these would be the right steps to take. But they are far from being a majority of the American people. The people of this country are badly divided on Vietnam, and it would be extremely difficult for the President of a democracy to lead his nation into what could become a major war without far stronger support for such a war than now exists.

The President has struggled to find a middle position between the hawks and the doves, but it is difficult for the nation to see where this is getting us and it is easy to see what it is costing.

Tying down a large part of this country's military force for years in a contest with an elusive guerrilla army and a minor Asian power, backed by the two major Communist powers, may endanger rather than strengthen the security of the U.S. Our inability to respond effectively even to provocation by North Korea illustrates this danger.

Here at home, the mounting cost of the war in lives and money is dividing and embittering the nation, exacerbating political and social conflicts, and diverting resources needed for the critical task of rebuilding American cities and other urgent programs. The attempt by the U.S. to avoid these effects — that is, to fight a war without paying for it — has already brought on domestic inflation and a crisis in the world monetary system.

Indeed, there is virtually nobody in this country who would not breathe a sigh of relief if this cruel, costly war could just be brought to a quick end.

Logically, one would expect this to be a prelude to a recommendation that the United States withdraw from Vietnam. If a given level of military involvement is both failing and at the same time endangering the country's "security"— that is, its power to intervene—elsewhere, then surely the only rational course is to liquidate the military involvement. Reducing the level would not help: it would only set the stage for worse defeats. And increasing the level would compound the weakness in other theaters, without providing any assurances of local success. Add to these military considerations the unfavorable economic and social implications of continuing the war—both domestically and internationally—and you have what seems like an irrefutable case for getting out of Vietnam.

And yet this is not at all *Business Week*'s conclusion. To be sure, it advocates negotiations with North Vietnam and the Vietcong; but it qualifies this by saying that "if in the course of negotiations, it became plain that the Vietcong was merely proposing to negotiate a U.S. and South Vietnamese surrender, the U.S. and its ally would be compelled to continue the war—until the Communists recognize that they are faced with a bloody stalemate, and have no hope of a military victory." Since "surrender," which obviously means withdrawal of United States forces with its inevitable corollary in the liquidation of the puppet Saigon regime, is ruled out, one wonders what the negotiations are supposed to be about. There is in fact no stalemate: the "Communists" are clearly winning. Does anyone imagine that they are now going to negotiate themselves out of the fruits of their hard-won military victories? *Business Week* and the interests for which it speaks are hardly that naive. The real meaning of the editorial in question must therefore be sought in the final paragraph which states:

If the U.S. government proves not only to other countries, but to the American people, that it is willing to do everything it honorably can for peace — "to walk that last mile," as the President says — it will command the support of the nation. And if every honest effort we make for peace fails, then the U.S. people must be prepared to back their government in renewed efforts to achieve, by military force, a settlement the U.S. can accept.

If we recall that only a few paragraphs earlier the *Business Week* editors had given it as their opinion that a "decisive military victory cannot be achieved with anything less than a massive new buildup of troops and arms in South Vietnam and an invasion of North Vietnam," then we must recognize that in reality it is precisely this course which they are advocating. Negotiations are thought of solely as a device for convincing the American people that there is no other "honorable" way.

We thus have the following paradox: While fully realizing the enormous costs and dangers of continuing the war, the editors of *Business Week* — and this also goes for practically all the establishment doves, including Kennedy and McCarthy — are not willing to advocate what they must know to be the only possible way of ending the war. We shall perhaps be told that we should not take this paradox too seriously — that anyone entering negotiations has to talk tough — that when it gets right down to the nitty gritty the relation of forces on the battlefield will be decisive, and that these relations inexorably dictate a United States withdrawal.

Perhaps it will work out that way. The American ruling class may yet be capable of learning the lesson that its wisest philosopher, Walter Lippmann, has been trying to teach it for two decades now, that the long-run interests of United States imperialism are not served by attempting to maintain a military presence on the mainland of Asia. If so, the first step would certainly be withdrawal from Vietnam (the question of whether and when to effect further withdrawals, for example from Thailand, would obviously not have to be made now). It must be admitted, however, that up to now at any rate Lippmann's ideas have attracted little support, and it seems likely that this may continue to be the case. Nor is this merely a matter of blindness or stupidity. For the truth is that the paradox referred to above arises not out of a mere transitory pre-negotiations situation but has profound roots in the whole structure of present-day international relations. The United States ruling class has at long last come to recognize the costs and dangers of *continuing* the war in Vietnam; but it is no less conscious of what it fears would be the costs and dangers of *losing* the war in Vietnam, which it now sees as the only possible alternative. In the words of the *Wall Street Journal* editorial from which we quoted above:

Should such be the upshot, that the U.S. abandons the effort not because it "should" do so but because its purposes have become irrelevant in the light of events on the battlefield and of Vietnamese politics, let no one blink the fact that it will be a disaster. It will be a stunning blow to the U.S. and the West in the larger struggle with international communism. At home it will be a traumatic experience to have lost a war in which thousands of Americans died in vain.

The editors of *Business Week* express essentially the same fears:

It is one thing to despise the war in Vietnam; but the U.S. is still committed not only there but in other parts of the Pacific, in Western Europe, in the Middle East, in Latin America. Vietnam must not be permitted to become the Achilles heel of a great nation; the U.S. must avoid a cut-and-run retreat from Vietnam that could not only lead quickly to wider disasters and losses abroad, but might result in an extremely dangerous kind of American isolationism.

The implication of such statements, it seems to us, is plain.

While to continue the war threatens a variety of disasters, to end it by withdrawing from Vietnam threatens the supreme disaster which can befall American imperialism: disintegration of its control over the "free world." More than three years ago Cyrus Sulzberger, the foreign affairs columnist of the *New York Times*, wrote: "The heart of the crisis is not truly in Vietnam. The quintessential problem is how to defeat revolutionary warfare." (March 3, 1965) Getting out of Vietnam now would be tantamount to confessing that this problem cannot be solved, that revolutionary warfare conducted by a completely dedicated people cannot be defeated. And that would be the beginning of the end not only of the American Empire but of the age of empires in general. Is it really credible that the United States ruling class will, by its own deliberate act, precipitate an historic turning point with such fateful implications for its own future? Is it not more likely that it will persist to the bitter end in its search for a way to defeat revolutionary warfare in Vietnam and thus to preserve for a while longer its grip on its threatened empire?

In implying an affirmative answer to this last question we do not mean to suggest that the search for a way to defeat revolutionary warfare in Vietnam can succeed. On the contrary, we believe that it is doomed to failure, that sooner or later the United States will be literally thrown out of Vietnam.* But it does not appear that that time is at hand, or that there would be much relevance to an analysis of the implications of an early peace in Vietnam.

The Meaning of Negotiations

While the politicians talk about peace in Vietnam, what really seems to be in the works is a bigger and more expensive war. In its latest (April) issue, *Fortune* has an article entitled "The New Arithmetic of Defense" which can be taken to reflect

---

* There are those who believe that rather than admit a military defeat in Vietnam, the United States would try to retrieve the situation through the use of atomic weapons. They should remember that the Chinese also have atomic weapons and that American military bases on the Asian mainland would be easy targets for atomic elimination. It is easy to talk about using A-bombs, but even the Pentagon's Strangeloves will think many, many times before deciding to do it.

current thinking among war planners in the Pentagon and Congress. A summary of the article, published in the front of the magazine, begins as follows:

> Hopes for a leveling off in war spending were among the casualties of the Tet offensive in Vietnam. We now have to take seriously the predictions that the U.S. buildup will go as high as 750,000 servicemen in Vietnam. At that level the war would cost an additional $9 billion a year (beyond the $24 billion a year it was costing at the end of 1967). A lot of that increase would go for personnel, helicopters, and ground ammunition, which the U.S. forces are now shooting up at the rate of $12,000 per year per enemy soldier in South Vietnam.

All of this, as Johnson's March 31st speech was at pains to emphasize, is supposed to go along with a big increase in the size of the South Vietnamese puppet army and its re-equipment with the latest weapons. And the entire package will undoubtedly be marketed in the United States as necessary to the building up of a position of strength from which to negotiate.

Here we can see with crystal clarity how "negotiations," which is supposed to be a peace policy, turns into a war policy in the hands of the defenders of the American Empire.* This is a fact which should be well pondered by all sections of the antiwar movement in the United States: to press for negotiations now is actually to help the warmakers. The only genuine antiwar demand is IMMEDIATE WITHDRAWAL.

Consequences of a Bigger War

Nearly two years and quite a few escalations ago, the Chinese *People's Daily* wrote:

> The 300,000 troops of United States imperialism have been badly mauled by the 31-million Vietnamese people. What can a few additional troops, warships, and aircraft do? To be quite frank, if United States imperialism kept its forces in Europe and Amer-

---

* It can be argued that Hanoi, by agreeing to enter into talks with the United States, similarly plays into the hands of the warmakers. But from Hanoi's point of view there is another consideration, namely, the political fragility of the Saigon puppet government. By agreeing to talks, it may be possible to hasten the collapse of the Thieu-Ky regime and the disintegration of the Saigon armies; and this obviously has to be a high-priority goal for both Hanoi and the National Liberation Front.

ica, the Asian people would have no way of wiping them out. Now, as it is so obliging as to deliver its goods to the customers' door, the Asian people cannot but express welcome. The more forces United States imperialism throws into Asia, the more will it be bogged down there and the deeper will be the grave it digs for itself. (Quoted in the *New York Times*, August 31, 1966.)

Since then more than 200,000 additional troops have been delivered, mauled, and bogged down, with the result that the United States is militarily weaker not only in Vietnam but everywhere else as well. Another quarter of a million will merely accelerate the process. And attempts to draft more men into the Saigon army and to give them the latest weapons will probably end up adding more strength to the NLF than to the puppet regime.

The non-military consequences of a bigger war are no less foreseeable. More military spending will mean at least the following: (1) A bigger budget deficit and more inflation, which in turn will lead to tighter money and pressures to cut back further on social services. (2) Greater disequilibrium in the balance of payments, triggering new international monetary crises. At some stage, possibly in the near future, the present international monetary system based on gold and dollars is likely to collapse and the "free world" to break up into warring currency blocs.

All this adds up to mounting economic chaos both in the United States and throughout the capitalist world. And the result can only be to bring to the surface and exacerbate all the myriad crises and contradictions with which that world is riddled. Inter-imperialist rivalries, revolutionary and national liberation struggles in the Third World, class struggles in both advanced and underdeveloped countries — all will feel the impact of the capitalist world's deepening economic strains. But the greatest effect, at least in the short run, will show itself in an explosive upsurge of that unique and irreconcilable conflict in the heart of the imperialist metropolis itself — the freedom struggle of the oppressed black inner colony.

During the whole summer of 1967 about a hundred American cities experienced varying degrees of racial violence. In the single week following the assassination of Martin Luther

King Jr. (according to a story in the *New York Times* of April 11), the number was 125. But King's murder not only touched off the national wave of uprisings. It also clarified the issues for many blacks who can no longer believe in a doctrine of nonviolence whose leading advocate has himself fallen victim to the very kind of violence he condemned. The mood of the black masses is certainly becoming more united and more militant; the summer which has begun so early in April must be expected to be by far the longest and hottest yet.

In the final analysis, as we have argued many times in these pages, capitalism has no solution to this conflict. No one ever decided to build ghettos and to crowd them with angry black people; no one decided to deprive these people of education and jobs; no one decided to treat them as subhuman, to oppress them with racist cops, to condemn them to a life of frustration and hopelessness. And by the same token no one can decide to undo these situations or reverse these trends. They are the cumulative consequences of millions of decisions directed to the seemingly unrelated aim of making as much money as possible by responding to the opportunities and penalties of the market — in other words obeying the most fundamental law of the established social order. But while capitalism cannot change its nature and abolish the contradictions and conflicts to which it gives rise, in the past it has shown considerable adaptability and skill in meliorating these conflicts — enacting reforms, buying off dissident leaders or even whole groups, providing enough crumbs from the capitalist table to blunt the edge of dissent and maintain a modicum of law and order.

It is here that United States capitalism has fallen down most glaringly and here that a large share of the blame can justly be charged to the war in Vietnam. There is scope for all sorts of reformist welfare programs which, if carried out with any imagination and determination, could serve to "cool" the militancy of the black masses. But these programs would necessarily cost a lot of public money, and in the present circumstances an increasing proportion of what is available goes to the Pentagon to fight the war in Vietnam and otherwise defend the Empire. Thus at the very time when violence was sweeping the country in the wake of King's assassination, the

New York Times (April 9) carried a story under the headline: "U.S. Cuts Antipoverty Funds in Northeast Cities." And two days later it added details:

New York City is threatened with a 65 percent cutback in summer jobs for youths — from 24,000 for which it received federal money last year to 8,400 this summer.

The threatened reduction was made known yesterday in a memorandum by Senator Jacob K. Javits, who said the projected cuts in federal aid elsewhere would drop Chicago summer youth jobs from 20,000 to 9,000, Washington from 7,000 to 2,000, Detroit from 2,750 to 2,000, and Dallas from 1,454 to 600.

With things going the way they are now, such apparent insanities must be expected to multiply. A losing war must be fought, a crumbling dollar must be shored up, the laws of a dying system must be obeyed. And if one by-product is a race war of unprecedented bitterness and destruction, well, that too must be set down as another cost of preserving Western Civilization and the glorious American Way of Life.

The Irrelevance of Capitalist Politics

Peace in Vietnam may have a lot to do with who is elected President of the United States next November, but who is elected President is not likely to have much to do with peace in Vietnam.

They all want peace, of course, and some will promise it more persuasively than others. But they all want the kind of peace which would crown a victory they are farther than ever from winning. And it now looks as if they will continue to believe in the possibility of such a miracle as long as their armed forces are able to maintain themselves in Vietnam. Peace, in other words, will come when those forces have been routed and must withdraw. And when that time comes it will not matter much who sits in the White House or which capitalist party controls the Congress.

In the meanwhile — and it may be a long while — the real issue of power in American capitalism is likely to be concerned less with personalities (McCarthy vs. Kennedy, Nixon vs. Rockefeller, etc.) or parties (Democrats vs. Republicans) and more with the role of the military. Bourgeoisies in trouble frequently look for salvation to the military, and frustrated armies frequently seek to install themselves in power. In the United States today we have a bourgeoisie in trouble — about that there is not likely to be much argument — and a military which is not only frustrated in Vietnam but also being called upon to play an increasingly important role in the domestic life of the country. ("All told," says *Business Week* of April 13th, "an estimated 21,000 federal troops and 45,000 national guardsmen were still deployed in and around the ghettos of the U.S. at midweek, with thousands more ready for action if needed.") As the problems become more acute, the idea of imposing military solutions — as much at home as abroad — is bound to spread.

The forms and consequences of military takeovers have differed in different countries and under different circumstances. Nazism was one form, in which the military was allied with a fascist mass movement; Gaullism was another form in which the masses played virtually no role. Some believe that the experience with the most to teach the United States today was that of Japan in the 1930's when the country was engaged in an ultimately losing war of imperialist conquest and the military seized the levers of power behind a screen of constitutionalism. Our own past history does not offer many obvious clues as to possible or probable developments here, though doubtless careful study seeking answers to the relevant questions will be much more revealing than the standard history books. But in any case we are probably justified in assuming that a drive to impose military solutions on the United States today would find civilians on both sides, and would certainly not have much to do with the traditional divisions and quarrels of American bourgeois politics.

A Japanese friend of ours, a leading authority on urban affairs, came to the United States a few months ago for the first time in several years. Shocked by the extent and speed of the changes he saw all around him, he wrote us a letter containing the following passage:

I never dreamed of the possibility of King's assassination. His teaching on nonviolence is sweet and acceptable words for American rulers, and I believed he was rather protected by them. Ever such a man was assassinated! The fact seems more serious than Kennedy's death and reminds me of the atmosphere in Japan in 1931-1940. The war in Manchuria was stalemated, and right-wing fascists attacked even middle-of-the-road liberals. We must expect a real hot long summer this year. Probably we may see the last stage of American Capitalism.

We would amend this in only one way: we *are* seeing the last stage of American capitalism. It may last a long time, but that fact should not be allowed to give rise to illusions. The only way this stage of capitalism can end is through a socialist revolution. Until then we shall live in a perpetual state of crisis and catastrophe. Any political perspective which denies or ignores this basic truth of our age is doomed to irrelevance.

Endless War

A report from Washington in the *New York Times* of March 8 states:

A State Department official who recently returned from speaking engagements at a number of universities was amazed that the students, who only six months ago were lambasting Washington for its Vietnam policy, hardly brought the subject up. Public pressure over the war has almost disappeared.

This surely remarkable state of affairs has obviously not been brought about because the fighting has stopped or even, on the average, greatly diminished. Casualties have been consistently over 200 Americans killed every week, and as we write in early March they are running around twice that figure. Nor is there any reason to believe that the reason is that people generally, and those who were previously such vocal protesters against the war in particular, have suddenly become convinced that the war is any more deserving of their support than it was a year ago. In this respect absolutely nothing has changed. What then is the reason?

Evidently that the American public, including most of the Left, expects that the Paris talks are really going to lead to a negotiated settlement in the reasonably near future.

The basis of this expectation is not the same for everyone. Probably a majority of the people believe what the government tells them, that it is earnestly seeking peace and that the military situation is such that the other side has no choice but to accept what Washington calls an "honorable" settlement. On this interpretation, the dragging out of the negotiations is due to the Communists' hope of winning at Paris what they have not been able to win on the battlefield. When they are convinced that this is impossible, they will be ready for an acceptable compromise.

Very few people on the Left, however, can base their expectation of an early end to the war on such grounds. The Left has learned to distrust just about everything the government says about Vietnam; for the most part it knows that what Washington has all along called an "honorable" peace means the maintenance of a neocolonial puppet regime in South Vietnam; and it also knows that it is precisely this noncompromisable issue of neocolonialism versus national liberation which has been at the heart of the struggle from the very beginning. On what, then, does the Left base its expectation of an early end?

The answer seems to be that the Left, or at any rate that part of it which until recently constituted the core of the antiwar movement, is convinced of two things: (1) that the continuation of the war is causing increasingly serious damage to the vital interests of the U.S. ruling class, undermining the international position of the dollar, and squandering resources which might be used to allay the country's mounting racial and urban crises; and (2) that the ruling class always bases its policies and actions on a rational calculation of what best serves its vital interests. *Ergo* the ruling class must want to end the war soon and can be expected to do so even though the price has to be withdrawal of U.S. forces from South Vietnam. A good statement of this position is given in Richard Du Boff's generally excellent review of Juan Bosch's latest book, which appeared in the April 1969 issue of *Monthly Review.*

The elders of the system . . . have clearly had enough. Wall Street, the multinational corporations, the foundation technocrats, the major news media, the international bankers all understand that the Vietnam intervention was essentially "correct," but that the tenacity of Vietnamese resistance was disastrously underestimated. The military and its civilian spokesmen sold them a bill of goods, and its cost has become unbearably high. The enterprise has got to be liquidated—and it probably will be.

The first difficulty with this theory is that it was just as applicable a year ago as it is now, and as a matter of fact it was freely used by leftists to explain Johnson's speech of March 31,

1968, curtailing the bombing of North Vietnam and offering to open peace talks. We were told then, too, that the ruling class had had enough and was about to throw in the towel. However, it must be recognized that a theory of this sort is not necessarily disproved by a lack of confirmation in a period as short as a year; its advocates can and do point to a variety of factors which may have contributed to the postponement of the expected action, and it is impossible to demonstrate beyond a reasonable doubt that some combination of these factors has not in fact played the role assigned to it. Those of us who believe the theory is wrong—and have so believed right along—must go beyond pointing out that it hasn't worked that way to an attack on the theory itself.

To begin with, we do not disagree with what was designated above as the first element of the theory in question: continuation of the war *is* causing increasingly serious damage to the vital interests of the U.S. ruling class. What is *not* correct is that the ruling class—in this country today or in any other country at any other time—always bases its policies on a rational calculation of what best serves its vital interests.

What are involved here are issues of great complexity which unfortunately have been sadly neglected by the social sciences. We have a plethora of studies of the *composition* of various ruling classes, but few if any studies of the determinants and dynamics of the *behavior* of ruling classes. In these circumstances there has been a strong tendency to substitute formulas and myths for knowledge and analysis. The ruling class is frequently treated as though it were a person, endowed in the same way with a mind and will of its own. Or it is assumed to have an all-powerful directorate which meets in secret to manipulate the levers of power. C. Wright Mills's theory of the "power elite," though seemingly more sophisticated, in reality is very similar in reducing class behavior to the behavior of a specified group of individuals. Once this reduction has been made, by whatever means, all that we know or think we know about how and why individuals act can be brought to bear on the problem of class behavior. And the result is quite likely to be all wrong.

This is not because classes do not act through individuals: of course they do. The error lies in assuming that people think and act the same way in their capacity as members of a class as they do in their capacity as private individuals. It is easy to show that this is not so. Take, for example, the question of a resort to violence. People who in their private lives would be horrified at the idea of killing another human being have no hesitation in advocating and participating in mass murder when they believe it to be in the national (i.e. ruling-class) interest. Nor is the method of conceiving interests and their relative importance the same in private as it is in class matters. Many illustrations of the kind of differences we have in mind could be given, but it hardly seems necessary in the present context. The single fact that people can simultaneously condemn murder and condone war is by itself enough to prove the necessity of a theory of class behavior quite separate from any theory or theories of individual behavior.

This is naturally not the place to try to present a theory of class behavior, but we do need to call attention to certain factors which would certainly enter into such a theory and without which it is impossible to understand the attitudes and policies of the U.S. ruling class toward Vietnam.

First, every ruling class *necessarily* generates an ideology —in the specific sense of an ensemble of ideas and morals and rationalizations—which serves to justify and legitimize its privileges and power. Much of this ideology is what Engels seems to have been the first to call "false consciousness": it misrepresents or distorts reality in order to convince exploited classes and peoples of the justice and inevitability of their fate. But, and this is the decisive point from our present angle of vision, it also and equally necessarily impairs the ability of the ruling class in question (and its assorted educators and publicists) to understand the historical situation in which it has its being.

Second, the fact that it does have its being in a given historical context means that the policies it devises and the actions it takes to protect and promote its interests depend in a crucially important way on its necessarily faulty interpretation of the dominant historical forces and trends of its epoch.

If the foregoing propositions are accepted, it follows that it can only be misleading to suppose that a ruling class can, still less that it actually does, base its actions on a rational calculation of what is likely to serve its interests most effectively —in the manner, say, of a businessman deciding on the basis of cost and market data whether or not to bring out a new line of products.

This is not to imply that a ruling class is ignorant of its interests. Its highest and, in case of conflict, overriding interest is preservation of the system in which its power and privileges are rooted; and in the case of most ruling classes scarcely lower priority is accorded to the expansion of that system. What we are saying is that pursuit of these goals involves dealing not with measurable data such as costs and prices and profits but rather with historic forces and trends which can never be traced and foreseen, even by the best of analysts, except within fairly wide limits, and which are bound to be interpreted by ruling classes with varying degrees of ideological error. It is therefore entirely wrong to assume that ruling-class policies are formulated on the basis of a rational and reliable comprehension of the realities of a given situation. The truth is that these policies can be understood and anticipated only through analyzing and making full allowance for the elements of error and irrationality which enter into them.

There are two further factors which have to be taken into account in dealing with ruling-class behavior. The first is the tremendous importance of what may be called momentum. When a certain decision is taken and a corresponding course of action is embarked upon, it may at first be done in a tentative and readily reversible way. But the longer it is persisted in and the wider and deeper the commitments which come to be involved, the harder it is to call a halt or turn aside. The second factor is the familiar one of "face." Ruling classes by definition are concerned with power, and power is a complicated phenomenon. It certainly does, in Chairman Mao's words, grow out of the barrel of a gun, but its extent and durability are affected by other factors, such as ability to satisfy people's needs, to overawe them, to command their admiration or respect. And in this complex, face—itself a mixture of success, credibility, and dignity—plays a significant part. The bigger a miscalculation and the more dire its threatened consequences, the greater is the motivation for a ruling class to try to recoup rather than admit it was wrong. In some circumstances, to be sure, the reason for wanting to save face may be merely false pride; but this is by no means always the case: the loss of face stemming from a serious defeat can dangerously undermine the power of a ruling class.

Before considering the U.S. involvement in Vietnam in the light of these observations on factors entering into the determination of ruling-class behavior, we want to emphasize a point which is perhaps obvious enough but which nevertheless is too often overlooked or neglected: History is full of examples of ruling classes which have failed to find their way out of crises and have consequently suffered terrible, and often fatal, disasters. And in many cases—perhaps even in all cases—there were prominent members of the doomed class who could clearly read the handwriting on the wall and yet were either unwilling or unable to intervene to alter the course of events. Only think of Germany in the first half of the twentieth century! Twice within a period of twenty-five years the German ruling class embarked on a career of unbridled conquest and expansion, and twice it suffered total defeat. Nor is it only hindsight that enables us to say that both efforts were foredoomed. What the British historian A. J. P. Taylor says about the first would be equally applicable to the second:

There existed in Germany in the First World War forces which repudiated [the] program of conquest and sought an alternative. The first of these forces came from all those members of the "governing classes"—intelligent industrialists, skeptical generals, rigid Junkers, competent bureaucrats, [the Chancellor] himself— who believed that Germany could not win the war; but as a peace without victory raised even more terrifying problems than endless war, their opposition counted for nothing. They regretted, they lamented, they complained; but they acquiesced in every step taken to achieve a world conquest which they believed impossible.*

* A. J. P. Taylor, *The Course of German History,* Putnam's, 1962, p. 192.

Let us turn now to the problem of the U.S. ruling class's Vietnam policy. The original involvement, in the late 1940's and early 1950's, was ostensibly to help the French reassert control over their prewar Indo-Chinese colony, but its real long-run purpose was undoubtedly to enable the Americans to replace the French as overlords in that part of the world. After the French defeat and withdrawal in 1954, the U.S. decided to settle for a Korea-type division of Vietnam, installing a neo-colonial puppet regime in Saigon and contemptuously flouting the Geneva accords which had brought the fighting to an end. This decision and the subsequent efforts to make it stick were unquestionably based upon an ideologically conditioned failure to understand the historical realities of the Vietnamese situation. The Vietnamese were thought of as inferior "natives" who would either be overawed by U.S. power or welcome its protection. The revolutionary aspect of the resistance to French rule was merely the local manifestation of the world Communist conspiracy with headquarters in Moscow (later moved to Peking). Because of these and related misconceptions, the U.S. ruling class figured that it would be easy to establish and maintain in South Vietnam a strategically located center of American imperial interests for all Southeast Asia and the South Pacific.

Later the character of the involvement changed. The puppet regime degenerated and by the second half of 1964 was on the verge of collapse. Faced with the choice of getting out of Vietnam altogether or Americanizing the war, Washington took the second course. Once again, ideologically conditioned miscalculations came into play: surely American soldiers with their enormously superior equipment and firepower would be able to finish off the raggle-taggle guerrillas in short order.

That was four years ago, and the guerrillas are militarily and politically stronger than ever. On the U.S. side a process of disillusionment, the beginnings of which can be traced back to even before the Americanization of the war, has already gone far: the elders of the system, as Du Boff rightly points out in the review we referred to earlier, have indeed had enough and would dearly love to liquidate the whole enterprise.

But by now the factors of momentum and face, both of which militate against any settlement which would exclude the American presence in South Vietnam, have acquired formidable dimensions.

The thing about the momentum factor which is most interesting is that it rests in large part on interests which have been created and blown up by and in the course of U.S. intervention itself. It has frequently been pointed out by critics of the thesis that the war in Vietnam has imperialist motives and aims that when the United States got involved American business had almost no interests in that country or the surrounding area. That was true fifteen years ago, but it is no longer true today. Many U.S. corporations and consortia of corporations have moved into South Vietnam, including the two biggest U.S. banks,* some of the country's largest construction firms, etc. And during the same years, U.S. business and finance have invaded and spread throughout the entire area from Thailand on the northwest to Australia and New Zealand on the southeast. But vested interests in the Vietnam war are by no means confined to Vietnam and the surrounding region: after all, most of the $30 billion added to the country's military budget as a direct consequence of the war is spent in the United States and nourishes in greater or lesser degree most of the country's military-industrial complex. Add to these facts that many states and congressional districts are economically and politically tied up with Vietnam-connected largesse and that an enormous bureaucracy both in the Pentagon and in various civilian government agencies is geared to the war's continuation—add all this up and you can begin to appreciate the fantastic momentum which now weighs against any drastic shifts in ruling-class policy toward Vietnam.

The factor of face is perhaps even more important. In 1954 it would have been relatively easy for the United States to write Vietnam off, just as China had been written off as lost by the Truman administration in 1949. But from then on it has become progressively more difficult. The Saigon regime became

---

* See Harry Magdoff, *The Age of Imperialism* (New York and London: Monthly Review Press, 1969), Chapter 3.

a U.S. puppet and as such was the recipient of all kinds of open and implied promises of aid and protection: any failure to keep these promises could not but contribute to undermining the relations between the United States and literally dozens of puppets and clients all over the globe. Still it might have been possible to wriggle out as long as the U.S. military posture in South Vietnam was that of adviser and helper: it could have been claimed, quite correctly, that the South Vietnam regime had shown itself incapable of using U.S. advice and aid effectively and that this released the United States from all further obligations. But once the war had been Americanized the whole problem underwent a qualitative change. It was no longer a weak and shaky government of a backward half-country against the Communists but the mighty, all-powerful United States of America against the armed forces of a country with about 15 percent of the U.S. population and an infinitesimal percentage of the per capita income. For the United States to admit defeat under these circumstances—and we should be clear that withdrawal from Vietnam would be precisely that—would entail a loss of face on a scale the world has probably never seen before. The Chinese contention that the United States is a paper tiger would be proved to the hilt, and every radical and revolutionary movement around the world would be encouraged to believe that what had been accomplished in Vietnam could, sooner or later, be duplicated everywhere else. Much as the elders might want to liquidate the war, they could only contemplate consequences of this sort with extreme misgivings and consternation.

We seem to have reached a situation now comparable to that in Germany during the First World War described in the above quotation from A. J. P. Taylor: as for the dissenting Germans of that time, so for our unhappy elders of today "a peace without victory raises even more terrifying problems than endless war." Only, for our elders matters are even worse, the alternative to endless war being not peace without victory but defeat. No wonder they opt for endless war.

And, make no mistake, endless war is the right name for the policy of the U.S. government today, as it has been for the past year. The issues in the "great debate" which took place behind the scenes in Washington during the month of March 1968—described in detail in two long stories in the *New York Times* of March 6 and 7—were not war or peace: they were escalation or continuation of the war at roughly the current level. And the decision went against escalation (and against the Pentagon) because the elders saw the prospects of success as dim and the costs in terms of vital ruling-class interests as prohibitive. But so far as we know, there is not a shred of evidence—certainly not in the *New York Times* stories—that anyone with access to the levers of power has at any time favored ending the war in Vietnam on the only terms it can be ended. Neither escalation nor withdrawal: this is a formula for endless war.

Not that endless war will really be endless in Vietnam any more than it was in Europe a half century earlier. It may therefore be useful to recall what it was that finally brought Germany to the end of her rope: military defeat at the front and rebellion in the rear.

We believe that it will be these same forces—and not costs or casualties or threats to the dollar—which will bring an end to the war in Vietnam. If we are right, the implications for the antiwar movement, and especially for the Left within the antiwar movement, are both obvious and profound.

What Next?

If it achieves nothing else, President Nixon's speech of November 3rd should at least have succeeded in destroying once and for all the illusion, so widespread on the Left during the last year and a half, that the U.S. ruling class has decided to liquidate the Vietnam war. Referring to the possibility of withdrawal from Vietnam, Nixon said:

For the United States this first defeat in our nation's history would result in a collapse of confidence in American leadership not only in Asia but throughout the world.

Three American Presidents have recognized the great stakes involved in Vietnam and understood what had to be done.

In 1963 President Kennedy with his characteristic eloquence and clarity said we want to see a stable government there, carrying on the struggle to maintain its national independence.

We believe strongly in that. We are not going to withdraw from that effort. In my opinion, for us to withdraw from that effort would mean a collapse not only of South Vietnam but Southeast Asia. So we're going to stay there.

Compared to this flat statement, Nixon's attempt to convince his audience that he has some kind of a "plan" to bring U.S. soldiers home from Vietnam—in one place he speaks of "all United States combat ground forces" and in another of "all of our forces"—is an obvious phony. The assumption underlying this supposed plan is that the Saigon forces can be built up to the point where they can "assume full responsibility for the security of South Vietnam." Yet it is clear enough from his own words that Nixon has no idea whether or when this might be achieved. At one point he said that "announcement of a fixed timetable for our withdrawal would completely remove any incentive for the enemy to negotiate an agreement. They would simply wait until our forces had withdrawn and then move in." But if Saigon couldn't take over the war by a fixed date, what reason is there to suppose that it would ever be able to? Obviously nothing in the historical record. And if Nixon feels so confident that it will be different in the future, one wonders why he thought it necessary to issue the following warning:

I want to be sure that there is no misunderstanding on the part of the enemy with regard to our withdrawal program. We have noted the reduced level of infiltration, the reduction of our casualties, and are basing our withdrawal decisions partially on those factors.

If the level of infiltration or our casualties increase while we are trying to scale down the fighting, it will be the result of a conscious decision by the enemy. Hanoi could make no greater mistake than to assume that an increase in violence will be to its advantage.

If I conclude that increased enemy action jeopardizes our remaining forces in Vietnam, I shall not hesitate to take strong and effective measures to deal with that situation.

Whether or not this is, as some have interpreted it, a veiled threat to use atomic weapons, it is certainly a statement of an intent to escalate the U.S. war effort under certain conditions. And it is perfectly clear that, in Nixon's own estimation, the existence or non-existence of these conditions depends not on Saigon but on the National Liberation Front and Hanoi.

One of two things follows. Either the talk about getting U.S. forces out of Vietnam is deliberate deception designed to cover up a policy of indefinite continuation of the war. Or Nixon thinks he can intimidate the NLF and the North Vietnamese into accepting the Saigon regime. The history of Vietnamese resistance to foreign domination over the centuries and more particularly during the last 25 years suggests that the likelihood of the second alternative is very close to zero, though this does not rule out the possibility that the lesson has not yet been learned by the American ruling class which has repeatedly shown itself capable of grotesque misunderstandings of Vietnamese reality. But it matters little whether Nixon is guilty of deception or miscalculation: in either case he has publicly committed the United States to a course which has been described in these pages on an earlier occasion as "endless war."

Once this is understood, the real meaning of the policy of "Vietnamization" which was so much stressed in Nixon's speech becomes clear. The purpose is of course not peace, and it is most unlikely that Nixon and his advisors really believe that they will be able to turn the war over to the puppet regime in Saigon. But they may nevertheless hope—through intensified training, provision of new equipment, increasing pay and improving living conditions, etc.—to be able to raise the fighting capacity of the Saigon forces enough to take some of the present strain off U.S. military manpower resources.

In this connection it is extremely important to understand that U.S. imperialism's greatest weakness is precisely a shortage of military manpower.* The Vietnam war is showing that the once-widespread hope of being able to substitute technology for manpower in fighting counter-revolutionary wars is an illusion. The United States has about 3.5 million men in the armed services at the present time (the largest military establishment in the world), and of this number at least a fifth are directly or indirectly tied down by a war in one small country many thousand miles away from home. Much of the remainder is spread thin over more than 250 military bases located in some 30 countries all around the globe. Considering the fact that the United States has arrogated to itself the role of world policeman—and Nixon's speech was nothing if not a reassertion of

---

* To say this is not to imply that a shortage of military manpower is the *only* weakness of U.S. imperialism. There are in fact many others. One, for example, is the unbalanced international payments position caused by huge outlays directly and indirectly connected with foreign military operations. Another stems from the lack of any genuine national solidarity at home, which prevents the government from employing the kind of wage, price, and fiscal controls necessary for the conduct of a smoothly working war economy. These and other weaknesses are responsible, along with a shortage of military manpower, for the incidents referred to in the text.

this claim—the present extreme dissipation of military resources brought about by the Vietnam war and the world-wide system of bases leaves a perilously small strategic reserve for deployment to new crisis areas. U.S. failure to react vigorously against North Korea's seizure of the intelligence ship *Pueblo* and shooting down of a spy plane obviously reflects this shortage of military resources, as does the increasing boldness of nationalist regimes in the Third World in encroaching on U.S. investments within their reach. Just in the last year Peru has nationalized properties of Standard Oil of New Jersey and W. R. Grace & Co.; Chile has moved on Anaconda's copper mines; a military coup in Libya has raised the specter of nationalization in what is now the world's third largest oil-exporting country; and Bolivia has seized the properties of Gulf Oil, by far the largest foreign investment in that country. And worse still is to be feared. The long-awaited Rockefeller report on U.S.-Latin American relations sounds an urgent note of alarm:

Throughout the hemisphere, although people are constantly moving out of poverty and degradation in varying numbers, the gap between the advantaged and the disadvantaged, within nations as well as between nations, is ever sharper and ever more difficult to endure. . . .

All of the American nations are a tempting target for Communist subversion. In fact it is plainly evident that such subversion is a reality today with alarming potential. . . .

Rising frustrations throughout the Western Hemisphere over poverty and political instability have led increasing numbers of people to pick the United States as a scapegoat and to seek out Marxist solutions to their socio-economic problems. At the moment there is only one Castro among the 26 nations of the hemisphere; there can well be more in the future. And a Castro on the mainland, supported militarily and economically by the Communist World, would present the gravest kind of threat to the security of the Western Hemisphere. (*New York Times,* November 10, 1969.)

Nor are external threats the only source of pressure on U.S. military manpower. Dissent and disaffection have been growing within the armed forces; and American youth, though still not resisting the draft in significant numbers, is increasingly shunning the Reserve Officers Training Corps (ROTC) which has traditionally been the main source of the all-important junior officer corps.* Clearly, the quality if not yet the quantity of internally available military manpower is declining at the very same time that global military and political developments are raising the U.S. ruling class's need for military strength to new heights.

In these circumstances "Vietnamization" can be seen to be an effort to squeeze more usable military manpower out of South Vietnam. To the extent that this can be done, which remains to be seen, U.S. forces can be released for service elsewhere or returned to the central strategic reserve. The purpose of "Vietnamization" is thus not to make peace but to enhance the capacity of the United States to make war everywhere else in the world.

This whole question of military manpower should receive much more attention from the Left, both here and abroad, than has yet been the case. Earlier capitalist empires, including particularly the British Empire of the nineteenth and early twentieth centuries, were able to control their dependencies and fight their internecine colonial wars without the use of conscript armies from the mother country. This was partly due to the relatively greater importance of naval superiority in earlier times, the weakness of colonial resistance movements and their lack of access to modern weaponry, and the recruitability of essentially mercenary forces among the un- and under-employed in the metropolis and in the precapitalist social structures of the periphery. These conditions began to change at least as early as the First World War which, together with its revolutionary aftermath, gave an enormous impetus to national liberation movements in the periphery. Today all the conditions of the problem have been transformed: for the United States now to

---

* Cutting down on the flow of new recruits to ROTC may well have been the most important anti-imperialist achievement to date of the student movement, though the more militant students on many campuses have tended to denigrate anti-ROTC actions as essentially liberal and pacifist. More attention to theory and its role in guiding practice would help to avoid such miscalculations in the future.

try to hold on to its empire without conscription both at home and in the satellite countries would be totally out of the question.

To continue this digression for a moment: The crucial nature of the military manpower problem was recognized by clear-sighted civilian and military representatives of U.S. imperialism during and immediately after the Second World War. They tried hard to take advantage of the war, postwar, and early cold-war climate of opinion to saddle the United States with a permanent system of Universal Military Training (UMT). But the U.S. bourgeoisie as a whole, faithfully represented in this respect by the Congress, preferred for a variety of reasons—political, economic, and personal—to buy the alternative theory of the substitutability of technology (especially airpower and atomic weaponry) for manpower. UMT was rejected and increasing billions were handed over to the military-industrial complex in a vain search for omnipotence through a combination of gadgetry and megatonnage.

Now the chickens are coming home to roost. Vietnam proves the need for manpower, and only the fact that other parts of the empire are for the moment militarily quiescent disguises the potentially fantastic dimensions of this need. At the same time, owing to the growth of the antiwar movement and the rising level of political consciousness at home, it is becoming increasingly difficult for the U.S. ruling class to fill even a part of its military manpower needs at home. Under these circumstances, efforts like "Vietnamization," i.e., the raising and training of hopefully reliable armies in the client and satellite states are certain to move higher and higher on Washington's agenda.

The Left should be aware of this. Military manpower may well turn out to be the Achilles Heel of U.S. imperialism. Everything that contributes to make the problem even more acute should be considered a step in the right direction.

Nixon's speech marks the end of one phase and the opening of another for the antiwar movement. Up to now, the great majority of its adherents have probably genuinely believed that sufficiently massive popular protests could cause the government to call a halt and bring the troops back home—after which, presumably, U.S. policy could be expected to be more prudent, avoiding further military entanglements and moving to adopt some of the reforms needed to allay the racial and urban crises at home. Underlying this perspective is the idea that Vietnam was a terrible "mistake" which has to be rectified before the country can return to a happier status quo ante.

That these were and are illusions has been argued, directly and indirectly, many times in these pages. The U.S. ruling class will change its policies when and if it feels its basic interests require it to do so, not because these policies are unpopular. And so far at any rate, as Nixon made abundantly clear on November 3rd, those who are now responsible for formulating and executing its policies feel that its basic interests require it to stay in Vietnam, not to get out.* An understanding of these truths should now spread far and wide throughout the antiwar movement. What are likely to be the results?

At least in the short run, there may well be a considerable number of dropouts and defections among those who had hoped to change the government's policy and now discover that the hope is vain. But much more important are those who will be angered and radicalized by the continuation of the war in the face of popular protests and in spite of the deepening of the country's manifold domestic crises. Here, we hope and believe, are the makings of a mass movement which is not only antiwar but anti-imperialist, which will know not only how to demonstrate against certain policies but how to oppose a system which inevitably generates such policies. In these circumstances it seems clear that a great opportunity beckons to the radical

---

* We do not want to be interpreted as holding that there are no divisions in the ruling class on Vietnam policy. Quite possibly there are influential figures who favor complete withdrawal on the best face-saving terms the other side will agree to. But one should not *overestimate* their number or importance. Many of those who now criticize Nixon and claim to be against the war do so for purely political reasons, acting in much the same way that Nixon himself did vis-à-vis Johnson. One thing is certain: the dread of the consequences of defeat in Vietnam is universal in the ruling class.

Left, that still small segment of the population which understands both the nature of imperialism and the role of the United States as its most advanced and dangerous embodiment.

It would be a mistake to imagine, however, that all will be plain sailing. The growth of the radical Left on the scale which now seems possible will of course be seen as a threat by the U.S. ruling class, to be met by the usual methods of demagogy, intimidation, and repression. But the particular situation which gave rise to and stimulated this growth can be expected to confer on the coming radicalism of the 1970's a specially menacing and sinister character in the eyes of the powers that be. For this new radicalism has its roots precisely in opposition to imperialism and war and hence can be expected, even long before it is strong enough to make a bid for power, to obstruct and perhaps even paralyze the war machine. And let there be no mistake: in the final analysis capitalism's way of coping with its internal contradictions as well as its external enemies has always been war. To threaten capitalism's ability to make war is therefore to threaten its very existence.

A brief excursion into history may help to clarify the issues here. Imperial Germany, emerging in the last third of the nineteenth century as the most dynamic imperialist power of the time, contained a potentially explosive mixture of classes and class conflicts. There were the traditional aristocracy, based mainly on the semi-feudal landed estates of the East; the big bourgeoisie rooted in heavy industry in the West; and a rapidly growing industrial proletariat. The interests of these three classes being profoundly antagonistic, the great problem of the Kaiser's Germany was to devise a way to reconcile them sufficiently to keep the society from tearing itself to pieces. The answer was found in militarism and imperialism. The aristocracy got agricultural protection and was assured dominance in a large and growing army. Heavy industry got armament orders and all-out state assistance in its efforts to capture overseas markets and to challenge Britain's naval supremacy. The working class shared in the process of rapid economic expansion and was both intimidated and bought off by a combination of repression and welfare-statism (both initiated by Bismarck well before 1900).

This system worked for nearly half a century, but at the cost of antagonizing both agricultural Russia and industrial Britain. Domestic contradictions were thus internationalized, with the well-known result that Germany was plunged into a two-front war and military disaster.

The German Revolution of 1918, being confined to the political level, brought no basic changes in the country's class structure: the agrarians, the industrialists, and the workers still confronted each other. Under the Weimar Republic, however, the workers were accorded a share of political power: and this fact, plus the restrictions imposed by the Versailles Treaty, precluded recourse to militarism and imperialist expansion as the traditional ways of reconciling internal class conflicts. For a few years during the 1920s a patchwork of compromises and half-measures kept the system going: foreign loans and technological rationalization for industry, subsidies (*Osthilfe*) and secret rearmament for the aristocracy, political rights and social welfare legislation for the workers. But with the coming of the Great Depression this patchwork of compromises completely collapsed. Weimar Germany came face to face with a profound crisis to which, given its economic structure and its political system, it had absolutely no answer.

There were two conceivable ways out. One was a social revolution which would transform the country's economic and class structure, the other a political counter-revolution which would allow Germany to return to its old ways of "solving" its problems through militarism and imperialist expansion. Unfortunately for Germany and the world there was never any real chance of a social revolution; not only was the working class divided, but neither of its political parties was prepared to lead a serious revolutionary struggle. Under these circumstances Hitler's National Socialism offered itself and was embraced by the propertied classes as the instrument of political counter-revolution. Historically, the deepest meaning of German fascism was that in a condition of stalemate it swept away the *political* obstacles to imperialist Germany's freedom to prepare for and wage war as the "solution" to its internal contradictions. But once again, as before 1914, the "solution" turned out to be but the prelude to disaster. Hitler smashed the independent economic and political organizations of the working class and, with the connivance of the British and French bourgeoisies which hoped to use him against the Soviet Union, tore up the Versailles Treaty. Rearmament and prosperity followed. But, as in Imperial Germany, the contradictions, far from being abolished, were merely transferred to the international sphere. Germany's revived and now insatiable imperialist ambitions soon brought her into conflict with a superior coalition and led once again to military defeat and this time the lasting partition of the country.

What the German experience indicates which is so relevant to our problems today is that for an imperialist ruling class the unfettered freedom to make war is absolutely vital to its continued existence. Anything which interferes with that freedom will be considered on a par with a direct threat to the system itself, to be dealt with by the full panoply of counter-revolutionary weapons, up to and including the scrapping of bourgeois democracy and the imposition of a fascist dictatorship.

The new radicalism in the United States is shaping up in a struggle against war and imperialism and will therefore necessarily, and rightly, do whatever it can to weaken U.S. imperialism's capacity to make war. What should be understood is that though it is not (yet) a revolutionary movement with a potential for seizing power, nevertheless it will probably be dealt with as such. And this in turn will both complicate the political tasks of the movement and open up new possibilities to it. It will be necessary to learn to combine *offensive* tactics against the system and its war-making potential with *defensive* tactics against the counter-revolutionary blows which will surely be unleashed.

Can the U.S. Left succeed where its German counterpart failed? No one knows, but one thing does seem sure: success will require a depth of understanding and a degree of political flexibility far greater than were ever shown by the German Left in its times of testing. One way to prepare ourselves is to study the lessons of history and do everything in our power to make them our own.

The War Spreads

Perhaps it is no more than a truism to say that wars either end or they spread: an endless war is a spreading war. But at least it is a truism which should not be ignored or forgotten. In his speech of November 3rd, Nixon talked about ending the war in Vietnam, but the policies he opted for were in fact designed to prolong it indefinitely. There should therefore be no surprise that now, just a few months later, the war is spreading and gives every evidence of continuing to spread.

Up until near the end of March the spreading process centered in northern Laos, which is sandwiched in between the bulk of North Vietnam on the east and Thailand on the west and south. Last year the pro-American Laotians, including a private mercenary army maintained by the CIA, captured the Plain of Jars, a strategically situated plateau more or less in the middle of northern Laos. This seemed to guarantee protection to the government centers of Luang Prabang and Vientiane and to constitute a buffer zone separating the North Vietnamese from northern Thailand, where guerrilla insurgency is under way but still largely isolated from outside support. All this changed quite suddenly in February when an offensive by the revolutionary Pathet Lao troops (supported, according to the capitalist press, by North Vietnamese) routed the pro-American forces and recaptured the Plain of Jars. This offensive evoked a response from the Americans in the form of heavy bombings, involving a large proportion of the B-52s in the Southeast Asia area. It was this stepped-up bombing which called attention in the United States to the spreading of the war in Laos and had its repercussions in Washington, especially in the Senate.

As usual, the bombings did not prove militarily decisive. The Plain of Jars remains in "enemy" hands, and it seems to be generally agreed, or at least feared, that the Pathet Lao and its allies can now proceed to take over all of northern Laos and link up with the Thai dissidents any time they choose to. That this is a setback for the Americans, with potential long-run consequences of far-reaching importance, seems clear. But there was not much the Americans could do about it. A look at the map is enough to show the impracticality of introducing U.S. ground forces into the area, which is 600 miles or so north-west of Saigon. Furthermore, an open escalation of the war at this time would ruin Nixon's carefully staged public-relations campaign to convince the American people that he is seriously trying to end the war.

It follows that a counter-move, to be effective, would have to be mounted elsewhere. And this may well be what accounts for at least the timing of the second stage of the spreading process—in Cambodia. The key move here was of course the overthrow of Prince Norodom Sihanouk as Chief of State, which took place on March 18th while the Prince was out of the country. Who wanted to get rid of Sihanouk and why? The Prince himself provided the answer in a speech delivered at the University of Paris several years ago:

The reason why we are opposing the United States is based on this fact: since 1955 the United States has tried various means, including the most treacherous and dangerous, to force us to join their side as a meek satellite. This is why we have carried on fierce resistance and spoken not very politely.*

Anyone familiar with CIA operations in such countries as Iran and Guatemala need be in no doubt about the nature of the means to which Sihanouk was referring: promotion of right-wing politico-terrorist organizations (the *Khmers Serei* or Free Khmers), suborning of political and military leaders with bribes and offers of generous U.S. aid, and so on. It was Sihanouk's

---

* Quoted in Keith Buchanan, "Cambodia Between Peking and Paris," *Monthly Review*, December 1964, p. 487. This article, while perhaps somewhat over-idealizing the Prince, provides much information of help in understanding the present situation.

great merit to have resisted all these efforts and thus to have spared his country and his people the twin horrors of war and American occupation. A dispatch to the *Washington Post* of March 14th, four days before Sihanouk's overthrow, made the point with dramatic emphasis:

"We could have had the billions of American dollars you see spent in Saigon, the skyscrapers and traffic jams of Bangkok, and the low-cost imported luxuries of Vientiane, if we had wished," said one government official recently. "But we also would have had, like those countries, American planes bombing our country-side, our cities filled with unemployed youths, a communist insur-rection all around us, galloping inflation, and an enormous trade deficit." (Quoted in *I. F. Stone's Bi-Weekly*, March 23.)

That these are precisely the blessings the new rulers of Cambodia are in the process of bringing down on their country hardly needs to be argued. According to the London *Economist* of March 21st, the new rulers of Cambodia have had a long-standing quarrel with Sihanouk:

Late last year they succeeded in launching a "new economic policy" opposed to Prince Sihanouk's system of state control. They clashed with him in December over a proposal to denationalize the banks. They believe that the economy has been doing badly ever since Prince Sihanouk rejected American aid in 1963. They will aim to secure new loans and a steady stream of foreign investment.

Here we have the tried-and-true formula for neocoloniza-tion and satellization, and it makes utter nonsense of the new leaders' protestations that their foreign policy will continue to be directed at the neutralization of the country.

As for the Americans, it can of course be taken for granted that a prime objective of their policy is—and, as Sihanouk's statement quoted above indicates, long has been—to integrate Cambodia solidly into their Southeast Asian empire. But, as is usually the case, a policy and the timing of its implementation are different matters requiring different explanations. Why did the anti-Sihanouk coup take place at precisely this time?

One obvious reason is that the Prince was out of the country. A head of state who has concentrated power in his own hands is much more vulnerable when he is away from the area where the power is exercised. This was illustrated in the overthrow of Kwame Nkrumah as President of Ghana, and it is confirmed by the coup in Cambodia. But absence from the country is not a sufficient explanation. After all, Sihanouk has made many trips abroad during his long years of rule, and up to now he has always managed to return unscathed. It seems likely that another factor was operating and that, given the domestic and international context, it played the decisive role. We refer to the urgent need of the Americans to escape from an increasingly untenable situation in Vietnam (and Laos).*

The nature of this untenable situation is of course well-known though not much discussed in the establishment media. In inheriting the Vietnam War from the Johnson administration, Nixon also inherited the danger of exactly the same kind of political death which struck Johnson down: *get out of Vietnam or suffer the consequences*. But get out of Vietnam he could not. The U.S. ruling class feels, with good reason, that defeat in Vietnam, which is exactly what withdrawal would be, would constitute a severe, and in the long run perhaps even fatal, blow to the whole structure of imperialist control over the Third World.** The ruling class is therefore not about to sanction, let alone encourage, a pull-out from Vietnam. What it does in effect is therefore to jettison an administration which fails to solve the insoluble problem of how to end the war in Vietnam while still winning it, and turns the very same problem over to a new administration, always hoping for a miracle.

---

* In speaking of "the Americans" this way, we do not mean to imply a belief that the various agencies and individuals concerned with policy making necessarily agree with each other or even know what some of the others are doing. The CIA, for example, undoubtedly enjoys a considerable degree of independence, and it may at times be able to create a *fait accompli* which forces the hands of those who are supposed to control it. But it is safe to assume that all those involved have pretty much the same conception of the national (i.e., ruling-class) interest, and that no course of action can be initiated and persisted in for long without the approval of the top policy-makers. We should therefore eschew "explanations" in terms of CIA-like plots and machinations, real though they are, and seek to identify the underlying interests involved in a given situation and the way the ruling class and its particular representatives and leaders at the time hope to benefit most (or lose least).

** For further discussion of this crucial point, see Chapter 9, pp. 125-134.

This was the situation which faced Nixon when he took office, and it must be said that during his first year he handled it with great political skill. By promising to "Vietnamize" the war and gradually withdraw U.S. forces, revising the draft system, talking about going over to an all-volunteer army, etc., Nixon took the wind out of the antiwar movement's sails. But he accomplished this neat trick only by seeming to do what he was in fact not doing, i.e., moving toward a withdrawal of U.S. forces from Vietnam. The respite was therefore in the nature of the case temporary, and the policy which produced it was certain to backfire as soon as its dupes woke up to what was really going on. In the meantime the poor fellow could only thrash around, vainly searching for a way out of the trap in which he was so firmly caught.

Under these circumstances it is hardly surprising that, in the words of a *Wall Street Journal* reporter, "the desire to 'do something' pervades top levels of government and may overpower other 'common sense' advice that insists the U.S. ability to shape events is negligible."* Where the "do something" urge takes over, there is of course always ready a rationalization to explain why the contemplated action is the very acme of wisdom, the long-sought key to victory, etc., etc. We have seen this process in operation at every major turning point in Vietnam for nearly two decades now: the Cambodian escalation is merely the latest, and unfortunately probably not the last, in a long, long series.

The rationalization this time is nicely spelled out by the foreign affairs columnist of the *New York Times*, Cyrus Sulzberger. Here are excerpts from his column (under the heading "Has a Strategy Collapsed?") of March 27th:

The key to Hanoi's effort to communize South Vietnam has been the technique of sanctuary warfare seeking to outflank and infiltrate the main target area from protected bases and supply routes in theoretically neutral Laos and Cambodia.

If the dramatic new situation in Cambodia can be made to stick, this strategy will come to a dead end. Cambodia, as ter-

---

* Robert Keatley, under the headline "Nixon Feels Pressure To Expand Role of U.S. in the Fighting in Asia," *Wall Street Journal,* April 3, 1970.

minus of the Ho Chi Minh Trail supply route across Laos, with its port of Sihanoukville for seaborne shipments to Hanoi's southern forces and as rehabilitation and reinforcement center for thousands of Communist troops, is crucially important. That is why Hanoi, Peking, and Moscow are all happy to help Prince Sihanouk attempt a comeback.

Sanctuaries are vital to modern revolutionary warfare. During the Greek civil conflict, Albania, Yugoslavia, and Bulgaria served as safe havens from which the rebels of General Markos were supplied and to which they could retreat. Only after Tito broke with Moscow, closed off his frontier with Greece, and isolated Albania, was Athens able to squash the insurrection. . . .

Saigon could completely pacify the delta and reinsure the capital's safety if Cambodia becomes truly neutral and ceases to serve as a base for aggression by forces mustered, commanded, and supported by Hanoi. . . .

What is evident is that Hanoi's system of sanctuary warfare is threatened, and unless it can be forcibly re-established there is a chance that peace can eventually be arranged in South Vietnam as it was in Greece when the Albanian haven was cut off.

It is not necessary here to undertake to expose all the fallacies in this pipe dream of the military and its journalistic apologists—to show, for example, how basically different the Vietnamese situation today is from the Greek situation of the late 1940's. But it is necessary to point out that Sulzberger's basic assumption—that the war in Vietnam results from "Hanoi's effort to communize South Vietnam," and represents "aggression by forces mustered, commanded, and supported by Hanoi" —is U.S. ruling-class mythology which approaches no nearer to reality through repetition. The main "enemy" in Vietnam is the National Liberation Front which is not going to go away or be pacified by the Saigon government no matter what happens in Cambodia. And as far as using Cambodia as a sanctuary is concerned, what reliable evidence we have suggests that it has not been anywhere near as important as U.S. spokesmen and pundits have claimed, and that the Cambodian government even under Sihanouk did its best to keep the practice to a minimum. Writing in the *Far Eastern Economic Review* (February 26), a correspondent reported as follows:

To get an idea of what the situation along the border was like, I travelled into Svay Rieng province [the region of Cambodia closest to Saigon], sometimes to within 500 metres of the frontier. Four things seem evident—at least as far as Svay Rieng province is concerned:

• The Vietcong use Cambodian territory much less than the Americans in Saigon claim.

• US aircraft violate Cambodian air space and bomb and strafe Cambodian territory in violation of the US guidelines, frequently with no cause at all, and much more often than the US admits.

• In fairness to all sides, it is obvious that the Americans, South Vietnamese, Vietcong, and North Vietnamese are all making some degree of effort to keep the war out of Cambodia.

• The Cambodian effort to hold ground against all comers belies any reports that they have an "agreement" with the communists— or for that matter with the Americans.

The editorial writers of the *New York Times* showed themselves to be a great deal more sober and realistic than Sulzberger when they wrote a few days after the appearance of his column quoted above:

The increased willingness of the Cambodian army under the new regime to permit allied cross-border raids against Vietnamese Communist sanctuaries undoubtedly strikes many South Vietnamese and American military men as a welcome opportunity. It opens the way to inflict more damage there on major Vietcong and North Vietnamese units, supply dumps, and headquarters. But it is also an opportunity to get bogged down on a new front that is unlikely to prove any more decisive than the battlefields already engaged. . . .

With 40,000 or more Vietnamese Communist troops in Cambodia, a huge allied military operation would have to be mounted if an effort were to be made to close down the sanctuary area. Even so, success undoubtedly would prove elusive. . . .

If some bases on the Cambodian side of the border could be rendered unusable, the Communist forces could move back a few miles to new bases. Or, if they felt seriously threatened in their sanctuary, they might be tempted to lend forces to Prince Sihanouk in an effort to restore him to power, a move that might bring an embarrassing request from Pnompenh for American military rescue. *Other possibilities can be imagined. They all lead not to ending the war but to widening it.* . . . (March 31. Emphasis added.)

This is certainly true as far as it goes. But it does not go far enough. What has to be understood now is that Sihanouk was the fulcrum in a precariously balanced equilibrium of forces. His removal has destroyed this equilibrium and released the forces which previously held each other in check. And the nature of these forces—the interests and objectives which energize them—is such that not only *may* they lead to a widening of the war, they *must* lead in that direction.

That the American and South Vietnamese military leaders want freedom to invade Cambodia is obvious. Hardly less obvious is the political interest of the Saigon government in sucking the Americans deeper into the Southeast Asian fighting. Perhaps not so obvious, at least as yet, is the fact that the new leaders in Cambodia have the same interest as the Saigon government in the deepest possible involvement of the Americans. As we saw above, they have deliberately chosen the role of U.S. satellite, which implies, in Southeast Asia even more than anywhere else in the world, becoming a military ward of the United States. As to the NLF and Hanoi, now that the old equilibrium around Sihanouk has been destroyed, their interest clearly lies in doing whatever they can to strengthen and hasten the victory of the revolutionary forces in Cambodia, as in Laos and elsewhere in the region. That these forces exist in the form of the Khmer Rouge movement is well known, though little information seems to be available on their present numbers or fighting potential. Another unknown at this stage is the future role of Sihanouk. Reports from Cambodia all agree that he was very popular in the countryside. What is unclear is whether this popularity will survive his overthrow and, if it does, whether he has the will and the ability to play a revolutionary as distinct from a conciliatory role. Historical analogies suggest a negative answer on both counts.

But in any case, speculation, even if it were well informed, on the strength of the Khmer Rouge or the possible role of Sihanouk would not go to the heart of the matter. Cambodia has been relatively sheltered from the ravages of war up to now. This immunity is coming to an end, thanks to the initiative of the Americans and/or their friends in Pnompenh. As the war spreads, the Cambodian people will be dragged into it willy-nilly and forced to take sides: either for national independence and social revolution, or for satellization and counterrevolution. It may take considerable time and experience for these issues to become clear, but when they do there is little reason to doubt that the mass of Cambodian people will, like the mass of Vietnamese before them, opt for independence and revolution.

When that time comes, the Americans will no doubt fervently wish the old Sihanouk were back in power in Pnompenh. But by then it will be too late. As has happened so many times before, and doubtless will happen even more times in the future, the United States, by seeking to extend its direct control, will have raised up and taught the very forces which fight back to achieve real independence. Reporting on his famous 1965 interview with Mao Tse-tung, Edgar Snow wrote:

During our conversation he repeatedly thanked foreign invaders for speeding up the Chinese revolution and for bestowing similar favors in Southeast Asia today. . . . He observed that the more American weapons and troops brought into Saigon, the faster the South Vietnamese liberation forces would become armed and educated to win victory. (*New Republic*, February 27, 1965.)

And now it is the turn of the Cambodians to receive American favors. May they make as good use of them as have their Chinese and Vietnamese brothers.

But these are the longer-term implications of the spread of the war into Cambodia. In the short run, in fact in the very near future, the most important consequence seems likely to be a major crisis in the United States itself. Nixon has kept the lid on by pretending to have a policy of getting out of Vietnam. This illusion could perhaps be kept alive for quite a while by soothing talk and small withdrawals of U.S. forces. But there is one proviso, that things should remain relatively quiet in Vietnam and the surrounding areas. With this proviso negated by the spread of the war, at first in Laos and now into Cambodia, the illusion itself must soon dissolve. And when the American people wake up to the reality that Nixon's policy, far from aiming at withdrawal from Vietnam, is to fight what Michael Klare aptly calls "the great South Asian war,"* the U.S. political scene could well be thrown into unprecedented turmoil.

---

* In an informative article in the *Nation* of March 9, 1970.

In a speech in the Senate on April 2nd, Fulbright said that the Communists "cannot drive us out of Indochina. But they can force on us the choice of either plunging in altogether or getting out altogether." Whether or not one agrees that it is "the Communists" who are forcing this choice on us, there can be no doubt that Fulbright has accurately identified the real alternatives facing the United States in Southeast Asia. The first alternative is clearly unacceptable to the mass of Americans, the second to the U.S. ruling class. Here are the makings of a crisis of world-shaking significance.

Modern Reader Paperbacks